# TRANSITION

## Principles for Biblical Parenting

BY:

Jennifer Parks

# COPY RIGHT

Copyright © 2025 by Jennifer Parks for 6Parks Media

All rights reserved.

No portion of this book may be reproduced in any form without written permission from the publisher or author, except as permitted by U.S. copyright law.

This publication is designed to provide accurate and authoritative information in regard to the subject matter covered. It is sold with the understanding that neither the author nor the publisher is engaged in rendering legal, investment, accounting or other professional services. While the publisher and author have used their best efforts in preparing this book, they make no representations or warranties with respect to the accuracy or completeness of the contents of this book and specifically disclaim any implied warranties of merchantability or fitness for a particular purpose. No warranty may be created or extended by sales representatives or written sales materials. The advice and strategies contained herein may not be suitable for your situation. You should consult with a professional when appropriate. Neither the publisher nor the author shall be liable for any loss of profit or any other commercial damages, including but not limited to special, incidental, consequential, personal, or other damages.

Book Cover by Lucy Banks

1st edition 2025

Library of Congress Control Number: 2025900594

ISBN: 979-8-218-59422-0

# TABLE OF CONTENT

Prologue ................................................................. i
Transition #1 *Conception*........................................ 2
Transition #2 Culture .............................................. 6
Transition #3 Consistency....................................... 10
Transition #4 The Kids are Here, Now What? ................. 13
Transition #5 Parenting........................................... 29
Transition #6 Coaching Through Puberty/Teen Years ..... 42
Transition #7 Collaboration ..................................... 48
Transition #8 Having done all, stand ............................. 52
Transition #9 End of the Road .................................. 60
Transition: #10 Trust.............................................. 75
Epilogue: .............................................................. 79
Anxious Thoughts .................................................. 82
Change of Heart and Attitude ................................. 85
Confidence ............................................................ 87
Education ............................................................. 89
Focus ................................................................... 91
Forgiveness .......................................................... 94
Friendship ............................................................ 96
Health .................................................................. 98
Integrity ............................................................... 100
Joy ...................................................................... 102

The Love of God ................................................................ 104
Laziness ............................................................................ 106
Mental Health ................................................................... 108
Money ............................................................................... 110
Negative Speech ............................................................... 113
Obedience ......................................................................... 116
Peace ................................................................................. 118
Relationship with Jesus .................................................... 121
Salvation ........................................................................... 124
Spiritual Warfare .............................................................. 127
Suicide .............................................................................. 130
Worldliness ....................................................................... 133

# Prologue

When I was a little girl, I wanted four things in life:
- To become a doctor
- To be a beauty queen with Pocahontas-length hair
- To live happily ever after with my very own Prince Charming named JP (I'm not even making this up. Ask my sister)
- To be a mother of four. (2 boys and 2 girls-I had an entire plan for the birth order just in case my little ones were ever bullied. The older ones would always defend the younger ones)

**Career**

As a child, someone once told me I wasn't smart enough to become a doctor and I believed them. (Keep this in mind, as I'll revisit it later in my journey as a parent.) Despite that discouragement, I discovered purpose and joy as a nurse, caring for children during their most vulnerable moments. I may not have achieved the title of doctor, but whenever my wonderful friend Latishia calls me *"Doctor*

*Parks,"* it feels as though my dream has been realized in an unexpected way.

**Beauty: Fall 2001**

During my fourth year of college, I was asked to be a bridesmaid. I had a dress made for a wedding that never took place. Instead of donating it, I chose to wear it in a beauty pageant. While most women might have given the dress away, I grew up glued to every televised beauty pageant. Naturally, I thought, "What should I do with an extra dress? Of course, enter a pageant!" I was always drawn to the world of beauty queens. I entered the competition for Miss USA Illinois, but I lost because I wore a color that was apparently forbidden red. Who knew red was off-limits in pageants back then? Not me! Despite all those years of watching, I had no idea.

Fast forward to 2012, I competed for the title of Mrs. Black Illinois Universe and won.

**Love: July 28, 2003**

My love story began in the most unexpected way when I met my future husband at Enterprise Rental Car. He was the assistant manager, tasked with helping me find a car. It was a challenging morning I looked completely disheveled in mismatched clothes, flip-flops, and wet hair. Then, out of nowhere, I heard the Lord say, *"This is your husband."*

I looked up to the sky, bewildered, and said, *"WHAT?!"* I wasn't searching for a partner; my mind was consumed with frustration over my "new" car, which I had to return to the dealership. To complicate matters, this man lived in an entirely different state! Yet, six months later, we were engaged.

**October 14, 2014**

As I drove to get my marriage license, I passed by a farm, completely unaware that one day it would be transformed into the community where my family and I now live. At the time, I had no idea that God was guiding me to catch an unintentional glimpse of the land where my future home would be built on long before its construction.

**October 16, 2004**

We got married on a date I can never seem to keep straight it was the 16th, not the 14th. Despite my occasional forgetfulness about our wedding date, we've managed to build a meaningful life together.

**Fun fact: My husband's initials are *JP***

**Motherhood: October 2005**

I experienced two cycles in one month and then nothing at all the following month.

**November 2005**

After receiving two positive pregnancy tests, I was overjoyed at the thought of becoming a mother. Unfortunately, not everyone in my life shared my excitement. However, my co-worker Jill's heartfelt smile and our shared love for Zach Morris and Saved by the Bell made that moment truly unforgettable, creating a special bond between us that I will always cherish.

God blessed us with four beautiful ***daughters.*** Together, we are Jason, Jennifer, Jada, Jayla, Jenna, and Jillian affectionately known as the *"J Crew."*

And yes, the older ones do stand up for the younger ones except for Jenna. She's the family bodyguard

**I am still waiting on that Pocahontas hair…**

And now these three remain: faith, hope, and love. But the greatest of these is love.

1 Corinthians 13:13

To be a good parent, you must first offer unconditional love to the child (assignment) that God has entrusted to you
*Especially when you don't feel particularly fond of them*

**Transition** *noun*

1. The process or a period of changing from one state or condition to another.

# Transition #1 *Conception*

Transitioning into motherhood is not merely an event but a journey shaped by consistency, communication, and a child-centered approach focusing on collaboration and shared values. As a pediatric and NICU nurse, I believed I was ready for what lay ahead. Despite the physical demands of pregnancy, I embraced it fully, praying over my children and decreeing blessings over their lives, inspired by Job 22:28, even before they were conceived

**Principle #1 Pray for your children even before conception**

*Jeremiah 1:5 says Before I formed you in the womb I knew you, before you were born, I set you apart and ordained you a prophet to the nations.* "Ordain" means to officially order or decree something. Your words carry power, so it's essential to speak life into your children. What you say can either uplift them or hold them back.

I went into labor for the first time at 29 weeks and then again at 34 weeks. The second time, the doctors couldn't stop the labor, and in July 2006, I delivered the twins. Twin B came out coughing, gray, and was diagnosed with necrotizing enterocolitis (NEC), which meant an immediate stay in the NICU. Having cared for preemies with NEC before, I understood how quickly the situation could worsen, but I had faith she would recover. I stayed calm, prayed, and fully trusted that God would fulfill His promise to answer my prayer

The hardest part for me was leaving her there alone. I was also managing my own health challenges, including preeclampsia, but little did I know, my mother visited her every day on her lunch break.

The Lord answered my prayer, and within two weeks, both of my babies were home. Caring for twins felt like managing a two-patient assignment. I loved the infant stage, but when it was time for them to sleep in their own cribs, chaos ensued. My co-worker Nancy suggested I needed a schedule and that I couldn't simply put them to bed I had to *transition* them into it.

**Principle #2 Establish a routine**

*"For God is not a God of disorder but of peace"*
*1 Corinthians 14:33a NLT*

Jason and I decided to follow her advice, and it made all the difference. We began putting the kids to bed each night after a calming bath, followed by a soothing lotion rubdown and gentle massage. Then, we would read them a book, say a prayer, and finish with some relaxing classical music. No matter what we were doing or where we were, we prioritized heading home to stick to our transition routine.

This simple, consistent ritual brought much-needed balance and stability to our lives. It established a sense of normalcy and, to my surprise, reduced the chaos that often left me feeling overwhelmed. For the first time in what felt like forever, Jason and I found ourselves with moments to truly connect without a child needing to nurse. This breath of fresh air allowed us the space to enjoy each other's company again.

**Benefits of Establishing a Routine:**

- **Predictability:** Creates a sense of stability and reassurance for both children and parents.
- **Time Management:** Promotes efficient organization of daily activities.
- **Reduced Stress:** Helps to minimize chaos and confusion in day-to-day life.

- **Developmental Support:** Encourages the growth of healthy habits and supports overall development.

# Transition #2 Culture

In 2009, I discovered I was pregnant again. And, just like before, the initial reaction from the family wasn't exactly positive. At the time, my husband was unemployed due to the 2008 financial crisis, working on his MBA, and struggling with what we now recognize was depressions

As my pregnancy progressed, my body began to change in ways I wasn't prepared for, including developing unexpected allergies. Despite reading countless pregnancy books, I had no idea this was even possible. From the start, I approached my second pregnancy with fear. I knew how to care for twins and how to care for sick children. But what was I supposed to do with a healthy, single baby?

I believe that fear, combined with the hurt I felt from others' rejection of my pregnancy, shaped the entire course of my gestation. The reality we see isn't all there is. There's a spiritual world that influences the physical one. When you don't know who you are or, even worse, whose you are you end up settling for far less than you deserve.

Jenna was born full-term, and I was overjoyed. But the next three years were incredibly challenging. I struggled with postpartum depression and didn't realize it could last so long. When I look back at pictures from that time, I just want to cry for the woman I was. Therapy, along with my faith in Jesus, helped me through that dark period

**Principle #3 It's okay to ask for help**

*I cried out to God for help; I cried out to God to hear me. When I was in distress, I sought the Lord; at night I stretched out untiring hands, and I would not be comforted. I remembered you, God, and I groaned; I meditated, and my spirit grew faint. You kept my eyes from closing; I was too troubled to speak.*
Psalms 77:1-4*NIV)*

In the African American community, there's often a stigma around asking for help, especially when it comes to mental health. If I had sought more support, perhaps my years of pain wouldn't have dragged on as long as they did. I felt like a failure because I couldn't do it all. I'll never forget the first year with the twins. For that entire year, I had consistent help.

But on their first birthday, it was like a switch flipped the help just stopped. It felt as though a memo had gone out, and everyone disappeared. The toddler years were a real struggle. I found myself yelling far more than I should have. There were days I called everyone I knew, but no one answered. I'd put the girls on the bed and just cry.

Looking back, I now understand how someone suffering from postpartum depression could reach the breaking point and commit Shaken Baby Syndrome. Thank God I never got to that point.

Having experienced those struggles as a mother, I stopped judging the parents of the babies I cared for. While I'll never condone such actions, I understand how overwhelming it can feel when you just want the crying to stop. That's why, whenever a friend has a baby now, I make it a point to tell them to call me no matter the time because I want them to know they don't have to face it alone.

Asking for help is vital in motherhood and life, as it aligns with God's design for community. Here's why it matters:

- **Emotional Relief**: Reaching out to others eases feelings of isolation and stress, allowing you to connect with people who understand and support you in Christ.
- **Practical Support**: Accepting help with tasks or childcare frees you to focus on your children and take

care of yourself (a lesson I wish I had learned sooner).

- **New Perspectives**: Seeking guidance from others offers fresh insights and creative solutions for the challenges you face.
- **Building a Support Network**: Asking for help strengthens your community, creating a dependable circle that makes your parenting journey more manageable and fulfilling.
- **Encouragement and Motivation**: The encouragement of others boosts your confidence and gives you the strength to keep going, knowing you're not alone.
- **Prioritizing Self-Care**: Acknowledging your need for support helps prevent burnout and provides time for rest and renewal in the Lord.
- **Modeling for Your Children**: Teaching your kids that it's okay to ask for help shows them the importance of community, collaboration, and trusting in God's provision.

# Transition #3 Consistency

**B**y the time I was pregnant with my third child, you'd think I would have stopped worrying about what others thought. But this pregnancy brought such mixed emotions that I didn't share the news with many people until I was six months along. Being on bed rest made it easier to keep it hidden. I remember my friend Lisa asking why I hadn't told her sooner, and I felt a deep sense of shame.

The truth is, I was overjoyed to be having another baby, but I was more focused on seeking approval from others than on fully embracing the blessing God had given me.

**Principle #4 You can't please everyone so just do the best you can**

*Am I now trying to win the approval of human beings, or of God? Or am I trying to please people? If I were still trying to please people, I would not be a servant of Christ.* ***Galatians 1:10***

I regret not fully embracing that pregnancy. I regret having my tubes tied, thinking it was the right decision at the time. I regret stopping breastfeeding earlier than I should have. Those were precious moments with my girls that I'll never get back, and I wish I had savored them more. But back then, I was so caught up in trying to please others. I focused more on appearances on maintaining the image of having it all together than on letting my home be what it was.

I spent so much time stressing over keeping everything perfect instead of cleaning as I went and letting go of the pressure. I wanted to be the mom God had called me to be, but I got tangled in the expectations of what family members said I should be.

I didn't take the time to enjoy raising my kids my way. I let outside voices dictate how I should mother, and in doing so, I lost sight of what truly mattered. Wise counsel is valuable, but it's also okay to make mistakes and figure things out on your own.

If I could go back, I would do things differently. But since I can't turn back time, I'm choosing to be different moving forward. I'm learning to embrace the imperfect moments, trust my instincts, and enjoy the journey of motherhood as it unfolds free from the weight of other people's expectations.

Letting go of people-pleasing in motherhood brings many benefits that strengthen your well-being and your family's health:

- **Better Mental Health**: Releasing the pressure to please others reduces stress and anxiety, bringing you peace through Christ.
- **Increased Confidence**: Standing firm in your needs boosts your self-esteem and provides a sense of security for your children.
- **Clearer Boundaries**: Setting godly boundaries protects your time and energy, allowing you to be fully present for your family.
- **Better Decision-Making**: Free from worldly expectations, you can make choices that align with your family's values in Christ.
- **Stronger Relationships**: Building genuine connections rooted in respect and love fosters a supportive, God-centered community.
- **Personal Growth**: Choosing not to seek approval from others promotes self-awareness and teaches your children to pursue their God-given passions

# Transition #4 The Kids are Here, Now What?

When the girls were little, I dreamed of staying home with them and homeschooling. But every time I brought it up, I'd hear the same thing: "You're a nurse, why would you want to do that?!" Each time, those questions made me doubt myself. Looking back, I wish I had trusted my heart and pursued the path I felt called to. It hasn't happened yet, but every day, I'm working toward becoming a full-time at-home mom and embracing the life of a self-proclaimed trophy wife. Raising my girls has been far from easy. There were more tears than I ever anticipated, and I often found myself praying just to get through the tough days. Somehow, I managed.

I used to think I had everything figured out. My self-esteem was strong, and I genuinely believed I was handling it all perfectly. When they were babies, I limited screen time, got on the floor to play with them, and played classical music during tummy time. When they were toddlers, we sang songs, put on fashion shows and performances, painted, visited the Children's Museum, and built things out of cardboard boxes.

As they reached school age, I made sure their days were filled with enriching experiences. We visited museums, joined park programs, went on walks, exercised together, and created stories. We read countless books from the library, embarked on mini road trips, spent time with friends and family, and explored new activities. I truly believe my girls had a wonderful childhood.

But as they grew older, friendships and social media became more central to their lives, and everything started to shift. I thought I was ready for this new phase of parenting. I read all the books, sought advice from wise mentors, and convinced myself that if I could just get through the early years, puberty and the teenage phase would be manageable. But reality was far more challenging than I had imagined.

The whirlwind of hormones and mood swings that come with raising girls caught me off guard. I was not ready. With the twins, it felt like living in two separate worlds. One was like a mini She-Hulk, ready to make you run for cover, while the other seemed to cry with every breath. I thought that if I could survive that chaos, I could handle whatever challenges the next phase of life threw my way. But then life introduced me to the middle school version of Generation Alpha.

Once again, I was unprepared for this storm of contradictions an unpredictable mix of oil and water, fire and brimstone. Many days, I found myself sitting in my car, crying out, *"Why, Lord?!"* Once, while washing dishes, I broke down completely, feeling utterly hopeless. It was as if I had forgotten everything I knew about faith and all the promises God had made in His Word. In the middle of those hot tears, I suddenly heard the Holy Spirit whisper, *"This is your next book."* I froze, wiped my face, and stared at the kitchen counter in disbelief. What? Why? I was struggling so much how could I possibly write a book about it? Didn't God see what I was going through? How could I offer guidance when I was still stumbling through it myself?

It was as if the Holy Spirit calmly responded, *"I said what I said."* So, in that moment, I asked, *"What do I say?"* At first, I thought the book would focus on surviving the teen years, on getting through the chaos and challenges of adolescence. But now, I feel God is leading me toward a broader story. The whole story. Not just surviving the tough moments but embracing them, learning from them, and discovering God's presence in the middle of the mess and uncertainty. It's not just about the journey of raising my girls it's also about my own growth. It's about how I'm changing, even when I feel unprepared, lost, and overwhelmed. That's the story I've been called to share.

I'm not a perfect parent, but I know I try my hardest and love my children more than anyone else could. After giving birth for the second time, I struggled to connect with my child. The beginning was much harder than I anticipated. I blamed myself, convinced it was my fault. Now I understand it was postpartum depression.

She was a wonderful baby. She slept well and was adorably chubby from all the nursing. She grew so quickly that the pediatrician even suggested we limit her intake. When I told the doctor we hadn't started solids yet, she was genuinely surprised.

However, once we introduced solids, everything changed. This kid would only eat eggs nothing else. Picky eaters like those who won't eat anything but chicken nuggets or peanut butter are one of my biggest frustrations. I understand everyone has preferences, but there's a difference between having tastes and being that kind of picky eater.

When I was growing up, we didn't have the variety kids have today. My grandmother, Ruby, cooked the same meals repeatedly: beans and cornbread, fish with spaghetti, oatmeal, cake with jelly, and yes, more beans with cornbread. I wanted to give my kids more than I had, but in hindsight, I may have overdone it. I might have tried too hard to make up for what I felt I lacked as a child.

Take it from me get rid of a scarcity mindset before you have children. That mindset can make it difficult to say *"no"* when it's needed and lead to saying *"yes"* when it isn't warranted.

**Principle #5 No is a complete sentence. Use it often**

*Matthew 5:37 Let what you say be simply 'Yes' or 'No': anything more than this comes from evil.*

Looking back, I realize there are moments in my parenting I could have approached differently. I certainly wouldn't have given in to tantrums as often as I did. I believe that when I gave too much, particularly with my third child, it set a precedent. This daughter of mine is bold always has been and I sincerely hope she remains so. Yet, our journey together has presented challenges I never anticipated, even more than with my other children. Through these experiences, I have learned a valuable lesson: *"Loving her where she is."*

One morning, after a particularly difficult and chaotic preteen episode, I felt encouraged by the Lord. I thought, *"If I'm reading and advising others to pray for peace, why not pray for peace over my daughter?"* With that, I decided to anoint her head with oil and pray peace over her for the day.

As I entered her room, ready to bless her, I reached out to touch her head. She immediately screamed, ducked away, and snapped, *"Don't touch me! I'm trying to do my hair!"* Given my persistent nature, I wasn't about to let that oil be wiped away on a towel. *(It's worth noting how my intention to pray for her shifted into being about me sigh, I'm still a work in progress.)* I needed the oil to touch her head because I genuinely believed she needed God's peace at that moment. I anointed her and gently touched her shoulder to pray, but she jerked away roughly, telling me to stop touching her because she was busy.

Two things truly irk me: a picky eater and a child pulling away from me. I won't lie I was hurt. As my anger began to rise, I felt the urge to snap back, but in that instant, I realized I needed to pray for peace instead of reacting.

Fighting back tears, I watched her, struggling to keep my composure. I spoke slowly and calmly, reminding myself to control my emotions and not sin in my anger. It was a test of patience and love a moment to be the mother she needed, not the one my frustration wanted me to be. Ultimately, I realized that loving our children often means letting go of our own expectations and responding with grace, even when they push us away.

**Principle #6 Don't react out of hurt or anger**

*Be angry but sin not: do not let the sun go down on your anger, and give no opportunity to the devil. Ephesians 4:26-27*

I responded, *"I love you. I love you so much, and I will always love you, no matter how you treat me."* Then I walked away, feeling a heavy mix of frustration and sadness. I wasn't sure if she could grasp the depth of what I was trying to convey, but I needed to make it clear. After that moment, the Holy Spirit led me to Galatians 5, where I reflected on words that spoke directly to my situation. In verse six, there is a powerful reminder: *"The only thing that counts is faith expressing itself through love."* That verse stopped me in my tracks. I realized that no matter how I feel at any given moment, love should always guide my actions. Even when things feel chaotic, love must remain the foundation. This doesn't mean I cannot be firm, but retaliatory tactics have no place in parenting. Their brains aren't fully developed they don't know what they don't know. On the other hand, I do. I know that adding fuel to the fire will only make it grow.

Verse thirteen also caught my attention: "Serve one another humbly in love." This was a quiet call to humility. If I'm going to lead my daughter through this challenging time, I must do so with humility not reacting in anger or frustration, but with a willingness to listen and understand, even when it's difficult. Verse fourteen follows with the timeless command to "love your neighbor as yourself." Finally, verse fifteen sealed it for me: *"If you bite and devour each other, watch out or you will be destroyed by each other."*

That last verse felt like a warning. If I let the anger and tension between us escalate, it will only harm our relationship in the long run. I realized that in my frustration, I could be just as guilty of "biting and devouring" as she might be, and that's not what either of us needs. This was a wake-up call to break the cycle intentionally.

It's easy to feel shocked and frustrated when my almost-teenager acts moody, defiant, or even downright mean. But I've had to remind myself that her behavior isn't meant to hurt me; she's trying to figure out who she is and how to express her feelings in a world that can be both confusing and overwhelming. As much as it feels personal when she challenges my authority or lashes out, I remind myself that she's an individual still learning how to manage her emotions. She's growing and searching for her place in the world, and this process is neither simple nor smooth.

It reminds me of when all my kids were toddlers. They disobeyed, put random things in their mouths, stuck forks into electric sockets, and even climbed into the oven all as part of pushing boundaries, growing, and exploring. Back then, I found it easier to laugh, forgive, and help redirect them. I saw them as young children developing through trial and error. Why am I struggling now to see this phase as another season of growth and development?

This doesn't mean I tolerate disrespect or poor behavior. In our home, we adhere to the wisdom of the entire Bible, including Proverbs 13:24, which states, *"Whoever spares the rod hates their child, but the one who loves their child is careful to discipline them,"* and Proverbs 22:15, which reminds us that "the rod of correction imparts wisdom, but the child left undisciplined brings shame to his mother.

"These verses shape how we raise our children, emphasizing that discipline is an essential aspect of love.

As an adult, it's my responsibility to decide when to react with discipline and when to respond with understanding and compassion. The hardest part is sitting with my own discomfort especially when I feel hurt or misunderstood. I often have to pause and ask myself, *"What does she need from me right now?"* Does she need discipline? Understanding? Space to process her emotions?

I also need to pay attention to the things she doesn't say the silent cues. Teenagers often struggle to articulate their emotions, especially when they feel overwhelmed. Much of what's happening inside her is still taking shape, and she might not even know how to put it into words. At this stage, she's still learning how to process her feelings and reactions.

As her parent, it's my role to model the emotional maturity I hope she'll develop as she grows. I need to reflect the behaviors and values I want her to adopt not mirror her current struggles. By demonstrating patience, self-control, and kindness, I can guide her toward internalizing those qualities over time. I don't expect perfection from her, but I do need to actively show her what maturity looks like in everyday life.

Kids, especially as they grow, often say things without fully understanding their impact. They haven't yet learned the importance of speaking with kindness and consideration. As parents, it's our responsibility to help them differentiate between valid thoughts and those better left unspoken because not every thought needs to be expressed aloud. When they lash out with hurtful words, it's vital not to react emotionally to everything they say. These moments provide an opportunity to model emotional maturity.

While it's tempting to view punishment as a way to *"get back"* at her for misbehavior, that mindset doesn't serve either of us. Instead, punishment should be a constructive tool a time for reflection, accountability, and the development of better habits without the distractions of favorite activities or privileges. During these moments, it's crucial that she not only recognizes the consequences of her actions but also understands how to make better choices moving forward. True growth occurs not just through discipline itself but in how she processes and responds to it.

It's easy to talk about these principles, but the reality is much harder when you're hurt, angry, or frustrated by your child's words or actions. In those moments, it's important to acknowledge your feelings but it's equally important to process them away from your child, especially when emotions are running high. If I'm upset or angry, I need to step back and allow myself time to calm down before engaging with her again. Once I've processed my emotions, I can return with clarity and a calm heart, ready to offer forgiveness and continue guiding her with love and understanding.

Ultimately, this journey is as much about my growth as it is hers. Parenting isn't about achieving perfection it's about learning to love, listen, and lead with grace, even in challenging moments.

**Principle #7 Forgive and forgive often**

*Mark 6:14-15 For if you forgive other people when they sin against you, your Heavenly Father will also forgive you. But if you do not forgive others their sins, your father will not forgive your sins.*

My children have the ability to hurt my feelings daily. This might not be everyone's experience, but for me,

I'm more sensitive than anyone else in my family. I know some moms who brush things off with a casual "c'est la vie" or even respond in kind, throwing the hurt right back at their child. As parents, however, we can't allow our children to go on without correction, nor should we hurt them just because they hurt us. Why? Because we are the adults.

From birth to 18 (and honestly, up to 25), these years are a critical training period for our children. They are still figuring out who they are, learning to manage their emotions, and understanding how to function in this world. It's our job to guide them, forgive them, and teach them well preparing them for a world that will not be as forgiving as we are. This is the hard work of parenting.

Right now, my 14-year-old is the one challenging me the most in this season. Last night, I had a dream that deeply unsettled me. In the dream, a toddler was being attacked by a teenager. The teenager was cold and unfeeling, completely indifferent to the harm they were causing. I woke up at 3 a.m., exhausted but unable to shake the dream. I immediately began to pray.

During that prayer, I felt convicted. The Holy Spirit reminded me of something I had said to my teen the night before. I had been scolding her and told her she wouldn't have to deal with me when she left for college in four years. As soon as the words left my mouth, I felt a pang of guilt. What I had said wasn't just about her leaving it was about me counting down to my so-called *"freedom."*

I realized I was treating her absence as something to look forward to, rather than cherishing the time we still have together. Instead of genuinely responding with love and patience, I had let my frustration take over. I knew I needed to repent for those words and apologize. So, the next morning, I went to her and apologized.

Guess what happened? She ignored me and was dismissive. In the past, I might have let her attitude trigger a reaction. But this time, I chose to handle it differently. I simply told her I loved her, apologized, and walked away. I held onto the conviction I felt during my prayer, determined not to let my emotions undo the work God was doing in my heart.

Parenting is about modeling maturity, forgiveness, and grace. As much as our children can hurt us, we must remember that we set the tone. We are the ones who show them how to manage emotions, apologize when we're wrong, and respond with love instead of reacting with anger. Even when it's hard, even when it feels unfair, we keep loving, guiding, and preparing them for a world that will require strength of character and kindness of spirit.

Saying no, controlling anger, and practicing forgiveness are essential skills grounded in Biblical principles. They not only enhance your personal growth but also strengthen your relationships and spiritual journey:

- **Empowerment**: Saying no establishes your boundaries and prioritizes the needs God has entrusted to you.
- **Emotional Control**: Responding with peace instead of anger demonstrates wisdom and fosters healthier interactions.
- **Reduced Conflict**: Forgiveness releases you from the grip of bitterness, bringing the peace Christ exemplified.
- **Stronger Relationships**: Setting boundaries and extending forgiveness nurtures meaningful connections and mirrors God's love.
- **Increased Resilience**: These practices cultivate spiritual resilience, equipping you to face life's challenges with grace.

- **Enhanced Well-Being** Adopting these principles reduces stress and aligns your heart with God's peace and purpose.
- **Modeling Christlike Behavior**: Practicing forgiveness and self-control inspires others, especially children, to embrace a faith-filled life.

# Transition #5 Parenting

*Only be careful, and watch yourselves closely so that you do not forget the things your eyes have seen or let them fade from your heart as long as you live. Teach them to your children and to their children after them.*
*Deuteronomy 4:9 NIV*

Each of my children has a uniquely shaped personality, and over time, I've learned to parent each of them in a way that aligns with their individual temperaments.

Twin #1, for instance, needs time. You can usually address most things with her right away, but when it comes to helping her shift her mindset or process something emotionally, she needs space to work through it on her own. For example, one day, she came home crying, struggling to understand why not everyone who calls themselves a *"friend"* is truly a friend.

At that moment, I knew it wasn't the time for an *"I told you so"* speech. Instead, I held her, gave her my love, and let her cry on my shoulder.

When she was ready, we had a heartfelt conversation about the birth, growth, and sometimes, the end of relationships. I explained that you can be a good friend, put in the effort, and love deeply, but some people may not be capable of handling or reciprocating the kind of love you offer. I also reminded her to stay true to herself, make changes when needed, and be discerning when her efforts aren't being returned.

Twin #2, on the other hand, is very different. She's the type who needs immediate attention when something is bothering her. If you give her time to sit with an issue, she won't just let it go she'll overthink it, turning it over in her mind until it becomes much bigger than it needs to be. What starts as a small disagreement or frustration can quickly escalate if left unchecked.

With her, it's all about addressing things head-on, right in the moment, before they have the chance to fester. If I sense something is off with her, I can't wait for the "perfect" moment to talk. I've learned that delaying only creates more tension like a pressure cooker building inside her. She'll internalize the issue, overanalyze it, and by the time I bring it up, she's already worked herself into an emotional state. More often than not, the root problem is something small something that could have been resolved easily if I had addressed it sooner.

One year, she took on too many activities and an overwhelming workload at school. Instead of addressing the situation directly, I tiptoed around it, avoiding the uncomfortable conversation rather than stepping in to prevent what I could see was quickly becoming a stressful situation. I tried to help as much as I could afterward, but in hindsight, I should have acted sooner and recognized that she was taking on too much.

I'll never forget when she became so overwhelmed that she begged to stay home from school, just wanting to sleep and escape the pressure. Normally, I don't allow my children to stay home unless absolutely necessary, but in that moment, the Holy Spirit revealed that she needed a break or this situation would break her. Only then did I realize how exhausted and emotionally drained she was. She ended up sleeping for 18 hours straight. Her skin broke out, and she developed gut issues. I understood then that her excessive drive to perform wasn't just about academics it was a deeper spiritual and emotional struggle that should have been addressed immediately. Since that experience, I've become more attentive to her verbal and non-verbal cues, stepping in promptly when I notice she's overwhelmed.

With child #4, I've learned that I need to stay actively involved until a task is completed. As the youngest, she naturally requires more guidance than her older siblings, who are now more self-sufficient. When I first started this book two years ago, she needed a lot more hand-holding. At the time, I couldn't just give her instructions and expect the task to be completed on her own I had to walk her through almost every step. It felt like a constant effort to keep her focused and moving forward, but I knew it was part of teaching her responsibility and the value of finishing what you start. With an eight-year age gap between my oldest and youngest, I think I had simply forgotten that part of the parenting journey.

Over time, I've started learning how to step back a little. She's growing, and she's beginning to take on more responsibility. I'm learning to give her space to experience life and figure things out on her own, even though it's difficult to let go of that hands-on approach. It's a delicate balance between allowing her the freedom to try and fail while being there when she needs support. She's starting to understand that life isn't always easy and that not every outcome will be pleasant or as she expected. Through it all, I remain beside her ready to teach, support, and comfort her when things get tough.

It's a beautiful thing to watch her start to build resilience, to see her face challenges and begin to understand that struggle is a natural part of growing up. She's realizing that not every moment will be "nice" or comfortable, but she's becoming better equipped to handle those moments independently. As a parent, I've had to learn patience and to trust the process, even when it feels like she might need more of my involvement. I hope I'm doing a better job this time around. Always "hovering" was exhausting, to say the least.

My role is shifting from constantly guiding her through every step to offering encouragement and wisdom when she truly needs it. And though she may still need me by her side for certain things, I can already see the foundation we've built together starting to bear fruit. She's growing, learning, and becoming stronger, and I'll be here for her every step of the way.

I know I skipped over child #3, but my *"firecracker"* has taught me the most about myself through the experience of being her mother, so she deserves her own page.

With child #3, I'm learning to pay closer attention to what she's not saying and spend more intentional time with her. She's not quite ready for full independence yet. I had started to ease up on my helicopter parenting, hoping to give her space to find her own way. However, I've realized she's not there yet. Instead of letting go completely, I now test her in smaller ways. I give her just enough freedom to see how she handles things on her own, but if she stumbles or falls, I'm there to catch her and guide her back on track. Then, we try again, using the lessons learned from the previous attempt. It's a delicate balance, but it's where she is in her journey, and I'm committed to walking with her through it.

I thought she had reached the point where I no longer needed to check her homework, assuming she would complete her assignments on her own. At this age, I had already started fostering independence with the twins. However, I soon discovered that she wasn't doing her work. Whether it was due to negative influences or simple procrastination, the fact remains she wasn't handling her responsibilities. I mistakenly believed that since my mother didn't help me with schoolwork and I had to figure it out on my own, she could do the same. But she's not me. She needs more oversight right now.

As much as we're both tired of me double-checking her syllabus and asking daily about her homework, it's necessary. Still, there are days when I get exhausted and simply tell her to "be mature" and handle it herself. But I'm learning that while pushing her toward independence is important, it must happen at a pace that aligns with her readiness not my expectations.

**Principle #8 "Do what I say, not what I do" is false theology**

*When a man makes a vow to the Lord or takes an oath to obligate himself by a pledge, he must not break his word but must do everything he said.*
***Numbers 30:2 NIV***

I would tell her to be consistent, yet here I was, being inconsistent myself. Her grades would improve for a while, but when I didn't remain consistent, they would slip again. I'd check in on her, but after a few days, I'd stop always finding some excuse not to stay on top of things. I told myself, *"I'm helping her. No one wants to be micromanaged. She needs space to manage things on her own."* But the truth was, with four kids, a career, a husband, the house, and the rare 1–2 days a year that I cared for myself, I was tired of having to monitor her every assignment.

Then the Lord asked me, *"How can she learn consistency if she sees you being inconsistent?"* That question struck me deeply. I realized I wasn't just inconsistent with her schoolwork. I was starting and stopping my weight-loss journey every two weeks, failing to keep a regular cooking and cleaning schedule, and always running late. I was all over the place. Once again, Jesus "gently" corrected me in a way that stung just enough to make me realize I needed to change. It was one of those moments where His truth hit hard, but it was exactly what I needed to hear to grow.

I'm still working on being consistent in every area of parenting. My intentions are good, but the outcomes often fall short of what I hope for. The main reason I've struggled is that I've been overcommitting to things I simply couldn't deliver on. I've learned that if I say I'm going to do something, I need to follow through no excuses. If I commit to showing up, I must show up. And if I can't do something or don't want to, I need to be honest with myself and avoid obligating myself unnecessarily.

**Principle #9 Don't get distracted**

*The seed cast in the weeds represents the ones who hear the kingdom news but are overwhelmed with worries about all the things they have to do and all the things they want to get. The stress strangles what they heard, and nothing comes of it.*

*Mark 4:18-19 MSG*

I have a confession: I get distracted. More often than not, it's fear that pulls my focus. My fear ends up making decisions for me instead of my faith. I became so consumed with worrying that one of my children might turn out differently than I hoped or repeat the mistakes I made that I unknowingly started pushing her in that direction. When others spoke negatively about my children, I found myself agreeing with them. I was feeding into the same narrative speaking negatively about her too. (Since I have four daughters, it didn't matter which "her" it was.) I tried to control every aspect of her life in an attempt to keep her safe, but all I did was push her further away. I was distracted by the things I could see in the moment rather than having faith in the future God has planned for her.

But I've made a decision. No matter the eye rolls, the huffing and puffing, or the bad attitude, I will continue to love her, pray for her, redirect her when needed, and stand firm in faith for her. It's not easy, but I refuse to give up on her. I've learned that I need to course-correct calmly (as calmly as I can), confidently (trusting that what I'm doing is right and not being afraid to be stern), and early (addressing issues before it's too late).

Before doing anything, I went to the Lord in prayer. I laid everything out before Him what was happening, how I felt, and my need for His guidance.

In parenting, minimizing distractions and modeling consistent behavior brings countless blessings. Here's how it benefits both you and your children:

- **Enhanced Focus**: Giving your children your undivided attention (instead of focusing on fears of messing them up) strengthens your bond, helping them feel valued and understood.
- **Consistency in Parenting**: Acting with consistency sets clear boundaries and expectations, providing your children with the security to grow and learn God's ways.

- **Effective Communication**: Staying focused allows for meaningful communication, enabling you to listen with a heart of love and guide your children in truth.
- **Emotional Stability**: Consistent behavior teaches your children how to manage their emotions by observing how you rely on the Lord in stressful times.
- **Positive Role Modeling**: Demonstrating patience, resilience, and focus shows your children how to walk in the Lord's ways and reflect His character
- **Stronger Relationships**: Uninterrupted quality time builds trust and fosters a deeper connection, creating a space where your children feel safe to express themselves.
- **Better Conflict Resolution**: Modeling peaceful, godly responses to challenges equips your children to handle conflicts with grace and wisdom.
- This is the path I'm walking now intentional, prayerful, and trusting God every step of the way.

**My prayer is simple but heartfelt:**

*"God, this is Your daughter. I give her back to You. I will no longer worry or be consumed by fear. Show me how to parent her. Give me the wisdom and strategy to guide her according to her unique needs. However, you have designed her to be led, teach me how to lead her. Lord, please guide my words. I break agreement with every negative word spoken over her whether by me or anyone else and I speak life into her future.*

*When she was an infant, I was mindful of my words because I understood how deeply they could shape her. Help me return to that mindset. Help me not to be distracted by what I see right now. Teach me to speak life and influence her future for Your kingdom. I know we have both failed in this relationship, but since I am the adult, help me to get back on track so that she can, too. I believe her future is bright, and she is blessed. Help me to stand firm in faith when the storms of life come, rather than cower in fear. By faith, I trust that everything will work out for good because You, Lord, have said so. In Jesus' name, I pray, Amen."*

**Coach** *noun*

1. A person who teaches and trains the members of a team and makes decisions about how they should play.
2. A horse-drawn carriage.

*Verb:*

1. An ongoing approach to manage people.

# Transition #6 Coaching Through Puberty/Teen Years

*Where no counsel is, the people fall: But in the multitude of counsellors there is safety.*
**Proverbs 11:14 KJV**

After putting my ego through rehab, I have a newfound respect for the process of thriving through ages 12–18. I've made a commitment to be consistent with my word, doing exactly what I say I will do. For example, I've stopped looking at the homework situation as micromanaging and instead see it as an honor to help my highly intelligent daughter stay on track by checking her schoolwork. If it's 10 p.m. and she hasn't completed her work, we sit together until it's done. The expectation in our family is clear: produce excellence and submit every assignment on time.

To my husband and me, excellence means doing your absolute best. This may look different depending on the situation, but delivering your best effort is the standard in our family.

The question I constantly ask myself is: how do I lead my children safely into adulthood? They are in the backseat of the vehicle, trusting that I know the way and can get them there without incident. But the truth is, the only way I know how to do anything is the way I do everything through prayer.

During the bootcamp training years (ages 0–5), I was relentless in my consistency. I was on it during this phase! I disciplined them regularly, tailoring my approach to suit their age and needs. *"Drop and give me 20"* was a weekly mantra in the Parks household, and even as toddlers, they had to follow through. If they misbehaved, they were put in the corner and had to stand with their arms outstretched against the wall for 60 seconds nothing too harsh, but to a 5-year-old, it felt like an eternity. If they fought, they were put in the "big shirt" together and forced to reconcile. If they were mean, they had to apologize, hug it out, and tell their sibling all the things they loved about them.

No TV during the week only play and imagination. (This rule ended when Jill was two because, frankly, I got tired of Play-Doh everywhere and needed a break.)

During the home training years (ages 6–18), chores became a way of life not as punishment, but as a way of building independence. I always reminded them, *"The maid quit, so it's just us now."* We'd write down all the chores, toss them in a hat, and draw them randomly no changes, no complaining. They each had assigned days to clean the kitchen. My friend once gave me life-saving advice: if they missed a day or didn't complete the job by a certain time, they had to wash the dishes for the next seven days. It was hilarious to watch them race to finish before 9 p.m. because, if they didn't, a sister would inevitably appear out of nowhere yelling, *"She didn't wash the dishes!!!"*

Our system is far from perfect, and my house may not always meet my mother's standards. But at the end of the day, everyone in our household knows how to boil an egg, prepare at least two meals, sweep, mop, clean baseboards, do their laundry, tidy their rooms, take out the trash, and even change a diaper. They're learning the practical skills they'll need in life while also becoming individuals who understand responsibility, discipline, and the value of hard work.

It's not always neat or smooth, but it's real. And that's what matters. I think even Coach Prime would approve of my efforts. Parenting a teenager is a rewarding but challenging journey. Here are some blessings of engaging positively with your teen:

**Increased Independence**: Supporting their path to independence helps them grow in wisdom and responsibility, preparing them for the life God has called them to live.

- **Strengthened Communication**: Encouraging open dialogue helps your teen speak with grace and truth, fostering understanding. (I'm still growing in this—Lord, help me listen more.)
- **Building Trust**: A relationship built on trust allows your teen to feel secure in sharing their burdens and seeking godly counsel.
- **Emotional Growth**: Patience and understanding during this season help both you and your teen grow in emotional maturity as you walk through challenges together in the Lord.
- **Enhanced Problem-Solving**: Allowing your teen to face difficulties and seek solutions strengthens their ability to discern God's will and handle life's challenges.

- **Stronger Family Bonds**: Spending intentional time together in love and unity builds family ties, creating a home where everyone feels valued and connected.
- **Preparation for Future Relationships**: Guiding your teen with positive reinforcement teaches them godly social skills and prepares them for meaningful future relationships.
- **Opportunities for Learning Together**: Parenting a teen opens doors for shared growth, where both parents and teens deepen their faith, knowledge, and love for one another.

**Collaboration** *noun*

1. The action of working with someone to produce or create something

# Transition #7 Collaboration

**Principle #10 quick to listen & slow to speak**
*Understand this, my dear brothers and sisters: You must all be quick to listen, slow to speak, and slow to get angry.*
James 1:19 NLT

As my twins approach adulthood, I've realized that I need to listen more carefully and explain myself more clearly. They're at an age where they need to understand the reasons behind my decisions, so I strive to give them a clear explanation of my thought process. This is important because, as they mature, they're not just looking for rules—they're seeking understanding. At the same time, I've learned the value of simplifying my communication. Using shorter sentences and avoiding lengthy lectures helps me keep their attention. If I talk too much, they tune me out, and I lose their focus.

They want to be decision-makers alongside me, and I respect that. While I am still the parent and ultimately have the final say, I recognize their need to feel heard and to have a voice in our discussions. We don't have to agree on everything, but I've found that involving them in certain decisions helps them feel valued and respected. There are topics where we can truly collaborate, working together to find better solutions. It's not always possible or appropriate, but when it is, it teaches them critical thinking and reinforces that their opinions matter.

This approach doesn't work for every situation, but when it does, it creates an environment where we can resolve things without eye rolls, arguments, or raised voices. It's a way to achieve the results I want while also encouraging their independence and maturity. I'm still the parent, but I'm learning to give them space to express themselves and opportunities to think through things with me. It's a delicate balance, but one that helps us grow together.

Listening to your teenager brings many blessings, both for their growth and your relationship. Here's how (no seriously, there really are benefits)

- **Increased Independence**: Actively listening supports their independence, helping them become more self-sufficient and gain the wisdom needed for adulthood.
- **Stronger Communication**: Open dialogue encourages your teen to express their thoughts and

emotions clearly, building their emotional intelligence.

- **Building Trust**: A relationship rooted in trust creates a safe space for your teen to share their heart and seek godly guidance.
- **Emotional Growth**: Demonstrating patience and understanding during this season fosters emotional maturity, strengthening your bond in the Lord.
- **Enhanced Problem-Solving**: Listening to their struggles inspires teens to think critically and develop problem-solving skills, equipping them for life's challenges.
- **Stronger Family Bonds**: Engaging with your teen through shared activities promotes unity and a sense of belonging, especially during this transitional time.
- **Preparation for Future Relationships**: Positive interactions with your teen teach them godly social skills and relationship wisdom for the future.
- **Opportunities for Learning Together**: These collaborative years offer a chance for shared growth, where both parents and teens deepen their faith, knowledge, and understanding.

# Stand *verb*

1. Have or maintain an upright position, supported by one's feet.

*Noun*

**2.** An attitude toward a particular issue: a position taken in an argument.

# Transition #8 Having done all, stand

### Principle #11 Stand back aka Back Up

*Therefore, put on the full armor of God, so that when the da y of evil comes, you may be able to stand your ground, and after you have done everything, to stand.*
***Ephesians 6:13 NIV***

When baking a cake, you have to understand that once you've mixed all the ingredients together carefully following the steps and preparing everything just right you've done all you can. At that point, you have to place the batter in the oven, step away, and trust that the heat and pressure will do their work. You've selected the best ingredients, followed the recipe as well as you knew how, and if you're like me, you've even prayed over it. Now, it's time to step back, trust the process, and hope for the best outcome.

Raising our children is much the same. They will face their own pressures, difficulties, and uncomfortable circumstances, but it's our job to trust God to guide and cover them through it all. There are times when I feel like I'm doing everything I can as a parent, but then there are moments like this morning when I just want to cry and retreat to my closet. (Side note: I didn't realize how often I mention crying throughout my parenting journey!) Those moments remind me that I need to stand back and surrender them to God. As much as I want to control every detail, there are times when I simply need to let go.

This morning, as I searched for scriptures on consistency to try and "do better," I came across a verse that spoke directly to my heart. I know it wasn't a coincidence it was God leading me. At that moment, I realized that just as I trust the heat of the oven to transform my cake into something beautiful, I need to trust God's timing and His work in my children's lives.

**1 Corinthians 15:58**

*Therefore, my beloved brothers, be steadfast, immovable, always abounding in the work of the Lord, knowing that in the Lord your labor is not in vain.*

**Galatians 6:9**

*And let us not grow weary of doing good, for in due season we will reap, if we do not give up*

In this season of my daughters' lives, I've had to remind myself that I don't need to control everything. My role is to show up, be present, and trust that everything I've done and continue to do is not in vain. They need the freedom to make their own decisions, and I have to give them space to experience the "heat" of their own circumstances. It's hard, but I can't give up on them or retreat to my closet just because I don't like some of their actions. Even when things get tough, I have to step back and trust God to guide their steps, just as He did mine.

I made mistakes as a kid sometimes things worked out, and other times, they didn't. But by God's grace, I made it through, and I didn't turn out so bad. I have to trust that they won't either. It's like baking a cake: if you open the oven door too early or check too often, it won't rise properly. The cake won't form evenly because the chemistry and transformation inside need time to work. I can check through the glass, and if there's a problem, I can address it, but I've learned that the key is to trust the process. Waiting is challenging, but if I want to see a fully formed cake, I have to trust the oven, trust the timing, and trust that what's happening inside is exactly what needs to happen. It's the same with my children sometimes I just need to trust the process and believe they're becoming who they're meant to be.

Speaking of control, it's incredibly difficult for me not to try to influence where they go to college. I want them to attend a faith-based institution because I believe being in an environment where Jesus is at the forefront will help guide them. But they're focused on finding a school that offers the most fun and the best opportunities for learning, and I understand that too. I worry about them leaving home, being away from our supervision, and facing the temptations of the world. But I also know that God will protect them no matter where they go. I feel led to introduce the idea of attending a Christian school, but ultimately, I know I have to trust God with their future.

This whole college application process has been a humbling experience. I've learned the hard way that "reminding" them to fill out scholarship applications before the deadline doesn't always go smoothly. More often than not, it's led to heated conversations and slammed doors.

(Honestly, I've been the one throwing more tantrums than I'd like to admit.) But God's grace has shown me that yelling and getting angry isn't the answer. It teaches them that it's okay to lash out when faced with opposition and that's not the lesson I want them to learn. Proverbs 15:1, 4, and 7 have been a constant reminder for me. God always knows how to reach me, so I can, in turn, reach them. It hurts to realize it, but He's right, and I was wrong.

I need to lead by example being stern and consistent, yes, but also learning to step back and allow them to face the consequences of their actions. As they grow, they need to learn how to work through challenges on their own. It's a delicate balance of guiding them while giving them space to grow and trusting that God's plan for them is bigger than my desire to control every detail. *(Editing note: When we showed them the school bill, they texted, "I need to fill out more scholarships.")*

This was probably my hardest obstacle to overcome but it made our relationships better. Giving your teen space to grow is essential for their development, strengthens their relationship with and increases their reliance on the Lord. Here are some key blessings:

**Fostering Independence**: Allowing them the freedom to make decisions nurtures godly self-reliance and prepares them for the path God has set for them.

**Improving Communication**: When given space, teens are more likely to open their hearts, leading to honest and meaningful conversations.

- **Building Trust**: Respecting their need for space shows them they are trusted, encouraging them to share without fear of judgment.
- **Promoting Emotional Maturity**: Giving space allows them to process their feelings, helping them grow in emotional strength and wisdom.
- **Encouraging Problem-Solving**: Letting them face challenges on their own helps them develop critical thinking and deepen their trust in God's guidance.
- **Strengthening Family Bonds**: Providing space actually strengthens relationships, creating

opportunities for more meaningful and loving quality time together.

- **Preparing for Future Relationships**: Teaching them to balance independence with connection equips them for healthy and fulfilling relationships in the future.
- **Facilitating Mutual Learning**: Space creates opportunities for both parents and teens to learn from one another, growing together in faith and wisdom.

# **Road** *noun*

1. A broad path leading from one location to another, typically with a specially prepared surface for vehicles to travel on.
2. A sequence of events or a course of action that leads to a specific outcome.

# Transition #9 End of the Road

**Principle #11 I don't how/what to do**

*Trust in the LORD with all thine heart; And lean not unto thine own understanding. In all thy ways acknowledge him, and he shall direct thy paths."*

*Proverbs 3:5-6 KJV*

Boyz II Men had a song called "End of the Road," and sometimes, as a parent, it feels like you've reached that point with your kids. What do you do when you realize it's time to let them make their own mistakes? When they've resisted your guidance, lied, snuck around, kept secrets, and disobeyed? You come to understand that your season of direct leadership those 18 years of nurturing and training is drawing to a close.

It's a moment of surrender. You realize that, despite all your efforts, you are no longer in control. It's time to let go, trust God with their future, and allow them to grow, face their own challenges, and learn from their own choices.

This is when you lean into Proverbs 3:5-6: *"Trust in the Lord with all your heart and lean not on your own understanding; in all your ways acknowledge Him, and He will make your paths straight."* You can't rely on your own wisdom or grasping at control anymore. It's time to go to Jesus and say, *"God, I'm at the end of myself. I've given everything I have. There were moments where I could've done better, and I didn't, but Lord, I am empty. Please take this burden, fill it with your love, grace, and guidance. This child was always truly Yours, and I trust in Your promise from Proverbs22:6 that if I train them in the way they should go, when they are old, they will not depart from it.*

*"* For me, my girls are getting older, and honestly, I'm not sure what more I can do besides ensuring they have everything they need for college. I'll drop them off, help them settle in, kiss them goodbye, and walk away. They've been accepted to wonderful colleges, closer to home than I had initially envisioned. I always pictured them going farther away to fully step out on their own, but perhaps neither of us were quite ready for that yet. Deep down, I believe they could have handled it. But if I'm being completely honest, I remember being a hot mess myself when I went to college and I stayed close to home too.

At this moment, I feel God asking me, *"Jennifer, do you trust Me?"* And I have to answer, *"Yes, Lord, I do. You are all I have."* Worrying about them won't keep them safe.

Stalking their every move won't protect them. Lectures, discipline, and chores can only go so far. What goes further is the Holy Spirit. As believers, we know the Holy Spirit lives in us, and there is no distance in the Spirit He can work on them anywhere, at any time, no matter what they are doing. So, my prayers and my surrender to God will go far beyond trying to be a *"secret agent mom."* I'm learning to trust that God has them and release the outcome to Him.

The prayer point God has given me, and that I'm holding onto for this season, is rooted in Galatians 5.

### Life by the Spirit

*¹³ You, my brothers and sisters, were called to be free. But do not use your freedom to indulge the flesh[a]; rather, serve one another humbly in love. ¹⁴ For the entire law is fulfilled in keeping this one command: "Love your neighbor as yourself." ¹⁵ If you bite and devour each other, watch out or you will be destroyed by each other.*

*¹⁶ So I say, walk by the Spirit, and you will not gratify the desires of the flesh. ¹⁷ For the flesh desires what is contrary to the Spirit, and the Spirit what is contrary to the flesh. They are in conflict with each other, so that you are not to do whatever you want. ¹⁸ But if you are led by the Spirit, you are not under the law.*

*¹⁹ The acts of the flesh are obvious: sexual immorality, impurity and debauchery; ²⁰ idolatry and witchcraft; hatred, discord, jealousy, fits of rage, selfish ambition, dissensions, factions ²¹ and envy; drunkenness, orgies, and the like. I warn you, as I did before, that those who live like this will not inherit the kingdom of God.*

*²² But the fruit of the Spirit is love, joy, peace, forbearance, kindness, goodness, faithfulness,²³ gentleness and self-control. Against such things there is no law. ²⁴ Those who belong to Christ Jesus have crucified the flesh with its passions and desires.²⁵ Since we live by the Spirit, let us keep in step with the Spirit. ²⁶ Let us not become conceited, provoking and envying each other.*

**My prayer for all of my children:**

*Dear Lord,*

*Please help my girls understand that they are free in You. Let them show love to everyone through the power of the Holy Spirit. Guide them to walk by the Spirit, listening to and obeying His words of guidance. I declare that they will not follow the desires of their flesh, doing whatever they want, but instead will walk according to the Spirit and inherit the Kingdom of Heaven.*

*In the name of Jesus, I declare that our children will not indulge in the desires of the flesh by participating in sexual immorality, impurity, lustful pleasures, idolatry, witchcraft, hatred, quarreling, jealousy (resenting what someone else has), outbursts of anger, selfish ambition, dissension (opposing and arguing the doctrine of salvation in Jesus), division, envy (wanting to take what someone else has out of resentment for their success), drunkenness, wild parties, and other sins like these. Instead, Lord, please bless them with the fruit of the Spirit in their lives. Let there be love, joy, peace, patience, kindness, goodness, faithfulness, gentleness, and self-control*

*Help them know that their sinful passions and desires have been nailed to the cross and crucified with Christ. Since we live by the Spirit, let them follow His leading in every area of their lives. Lastly, let them not become conceited or provoke or envy one another.*

**In Jesus' name, we pray. Amen.**

I feel like this prayer covers it all. I don't have to worry because it addresses nearly every challenge I can think of, and my faith fills in the gaps. Of course, I'll continue to pray for their health, friendships, and prosperity, but ultimately, if we walk in the Spirit, we know we're protected. He is more than capable of handling whatever comes our way

At the end of this particular road, we must entrust our children to God as they step out into the world. But we don't simply let them go on their own—we equip them. Every transition in their lives is a new training ground, a fresh opportunity for us to guide them. And to do that well, we need discipline, discipleship, and discernment. I feel like this prayer covers it all. I don't have to worry because it addresses nearly every challenge I can think of, and my faith fills in the gaps. Of course, I'll continue to pray for their health, friendships, and prosperity, but ultimately, if we walk in the Spirit, we know we're protected. He is more than capable of handling whatever comes our way.

**Discernment:** When the Holy Spirit brings something to your attention, pause and pray immediately. Your prayers hold incredible power. They can alter situations and influence the direction of your child's life, no matter where they are or what they're doing. If you feel that the Holy Spirit is alerting you to a friend who doesn't have the best intentions for them, speak up. If you perceive that your child is heading in the wrong direction, guide them with love and **discipline** them in a way that reflects God's character (Proverbs 13:24). It might be difficult, but it could protect their life or shape their future. And as you do, ensure they understand that it's the Holy Spirit leading you. If they feel upset, that's a matter between them and God, but don't let that deter you from doing what's right.

**Discipleship:** Always make the love of Jesus and His presence known in your home. Read the Bible together and discuss how His Word applies to their lives right now. Live out the scriptures in front of them because they are watching you closely. What do they see? Do they see you reading the Word? Do they see you praying? Do they observe you living a life that reflects a genuine relationship with Christ, or do they notice something else?

None of us are perfect. We all stumble and make mistakes. However, our children should witness us humbling ourselves during challenging times, seeking God's forgiveness, and learning to do better moving forward. Above all, they should see us on a journey a journey of growth, humility, and a deepening relationship with Christ that consistently reveals His love in all that we do.

I don't claim to have all the answers. This is simply my experience of motherhood as I know it. I pray that some part of my story resonates with you and can be applied to your own life. Ultimately, our calling is to raise children who are focused on God's kingdom children who will go out into the world to make a difference, bringing others to Christ and creating disciples along the way.

Relying on the Lord brings countless blessings that strengthen our lives and faith. Here are some key advantages:

**Peace of Mind**: Trusting in the Lord brings a sense of calm, easing anxiety and reassuring us that we are never alone.

- **Guidance and Direction**: Turning to God for wisdom helps us make sound decisions and walk a righteous path.
- **Strength in Adversity**: Depending on the Lord gives us the courage to face life's trials, knowing He is our source of comfort.
- **Community and Support**: Faith connects us with others who offer encouragement and strength, deepening our bond in the Lord.
- **Moral Compass**: God's guidance provides clarity and inspires us to live with integrity and purpose.

- **Hope and Optimism**: Trusting in God instills hope for the future, helping us stay resilient through life's challenges.
- **Personal Growth**: Leaning on the Lord encourages self-reflection and a deeper understanding of His plan for our lives.
- **Gratitude and Contentment**: Relying on God nurtures thankfulness and contentment, bringing peace and joy to our daily experiences.

The week leading up to college drop-off was incredibly difficult. During that time, the Holy Spirit revealed so much about myself and my parenting. I realized how controlling I had been. I didn't fully trust Him to do what I needed Him to do. Instead, I would pray for God's help, but before I even finished saying *"Amen,"* I was already trying to *"fix it"* myself. My focus was so consumed by preventing my kids from making the mistakes I had made that I tried to control every aspect of their lives, all in the name of *"good parenting."*

Even as I write this, it's hard to admit. Part of me wants to say, *"No, I was just trying to help them in the areas where I wasn't helped."* It's true that being there for your children is important, but as I've said before, we have to let go. This week showed me how much I truly trust or don't trust the Lord to care for the children He gave me.

The lesson began on Monday when God showed me something about how I interact with my patients. I often try to convince them to follow the health care plan I've created, but many times, they resist. They either push back or outright disagree with the care plan. They want to do things their own way. For years, I've joked, *"I don't like adults because they don't listen. In pediatrics, the kids have to listen they don't have a choice."* I brought that same mindset into my parenting. I would see the problem, come up with the solution, and expect my children to follow it. And if they didn't? That was fine because either I would step in and do it for them, or I would find a way to persuade them to do it my way.

I genuinely want what's best for my children. When it comes to situations we can handle, I believe that as adults in authority over minors, we should do a lot but not everything.

On Tuesday, my child took her sweet time getting ready for the hairdresser and was about to miss the appointment I had begged to fit her into at the last minute. I tried everything explaining, begging, and finally scolding to get her moving. Looking back, I realize I should've let her miss the appointment and gone myself in her place. Experience, after all, is a powerful teacher.

Even at work that day, I tried a new approach. I offered my solution to a patient, explained why I recommended it, and when they declined, I simply took a deep breath, noted "patient declined," and moved on to the next patient. This was so hard for me. In my mind, I believed I knew what would happen if they didn't follow the regimen. As I started to write, *"I knew what would happen,"* the Holy Spirit gently reminded me: I don't actually know. He keeps humbling me. Although it was difficult, it wasn't an impossible situation, and I survived.

On Wednesday, it was "preview day" for my rising middle schooler. She struggled to figure out how to use her locker combination. The whole right-left-passing-zero-left process was unfamiliar and frustrating. I tried to help, but that only made her more upset. Her sister stepped in, but things got even worse. Finally, I asked her friend's dad to help, and surprisingly, it worked. He said THE EXACT SAME THING I had said, but we all know how it goes kids are more likely to listen when advice comes from someone else.

I realized I needed to step back and give her the space to figure it out on her own. I trusted that she'd learn how to navigate the halls and classrooms, especially with her friend showing her the ropes. I only stepped in when I noticed her heading in the wrong direction. I stayed nearby, though, so she knew she could ask for help if needed.

After that, my once-confident 14-year-old who hadn't missed a single eye roll during the middle school walkthrough completely shut down during the high school walkthrough. It was overwhelming for her, even though there were plenty of teachers, staff, and maps to guide us. She wanted nothing to do with any of it. I offered to help, but she firmly said no. I suggested getting a map, but she refused. I asked if we could ask for directions, and once again, she declined.

Determined to help, I went ahead and asked for directions anyway. When I shared them with her, she chose to go in the complete opposite direction.

At one point, when I could see she was on the verge of breaking down, I pulled her aside, reassured her that everything would be okay, guided her through some deep breaths, and reminded her of the victories we had already achieved that day. Then, I called in reinforcements her big sisters, who had just graduated and knew the school like the back of their hands.

The old me Monday morning's version of me would have taken over, grabbed the map, and insisted she follow my lead. But what would that have accomplished? I wasn't parenting a toddler anymore. I was parenting a teenager, and I had to adapt.

Transitioning with the twins had been easier because I didn't know any other way I simply trusted God and went with it. But now, after years of experience, I had started to assume that the same methods would work for my 14-year-old. The truth is, they don't. Every child is different, and what works for one doesn't always work for another.

When the twins arrived, I watched as my daughter's anxiety melted away. Her smile returned, and she was ready to start again. My youngest, however, was busy complaining about the stairs. I gently reminded her that this would be her reality in four years, so it was good to see it now. We followed behind the older sisters as they confidently led the way through the halls.

About 15 minutes into the tour, I decided that my youngest and I would wait for them in the cafeteria. As I sat there, the Holy Spirit prompted me to write down the lesson

I was learning in that moment. I couldn't help but laugh because He revealed a hidden disobedience within me that I hadn't even realized was there. I suppose that's what happens when you pray, "If there's anything in me that's not like You, Lord, clean it out. If there's a hidden way within me that I don't see, uproot it and cast it away."

In that moment, He tore down the idol I had made out of parenting, exposing how I had placed control and my own expectations above trusting Him. And I suppose this marks the beginning of the *"final"* transition...

**Trust** *noun*

> 1. Firm belief in the reliability, truth, ability of strength of someone or something.

# Transition: #10 Trust

*What time I am afraid, I will trust in thee. In God I will praise his word, In God I have put my trust; I will not fear what flesh can do unto me. Psalm 56:3-4 KJV*

The Lord created our children, and they belong to Him. We are simply caretakers of His estate, entrusted with the responsibility of nurturing His precious gifts. We won't always get it right, but if we refer to the "manual" He left us, we will find the answers. We can always call home (through prayer) for real-time instructions for our day-to-day tasks. Patience is essential as we wait on God's help. His answers don't always look like what we asked for, but they are always exactly what we need.

On Saturday, the day before college move-in, my four girls spent some quality sister time together at a fair. Although we didn't get to have our usual pizza and movie night as planned, it was heartwarming to see their friends come over to say goodbye. Move-in day itself was exhausting, especially with them heading to two different schools. Watching them part ways wasn't easy, but I'm confident their bond will only grow stronger from here. I'm still praying for their transitions to college.

The one I was most concerned about seems to be adjusting well, while the other is struggling with being away from home. She's encountering new situations and seeing people do things she didn't grow up around. I'm praying that her light will shine brightly in the darkness and that the darkness will not overcome it (John 1:5).

I've been blessed with the incredible privilege of being with them every day for 18 years. However, I didn't have much time to dwell on it because life kept moving. The youngest had tumbling practice, my 14-year-old had an activity, my husband needed something, my parents were coming over, and there was just so much to do. Life moved forward, and I kept moving with it.

Trusting in the Lord with your children's future brings great peace and hope. Here are the key blessings:

- **Confidence in His Plan**: Placing their future in God's hands assures you that He has a purpose and plan for their lives, even when the path seems uncertain.

- **Guidance in Decisions**: Relying on the Lord gives you confidence, knowing He will guide their steps and help them make wise choices.
- **Protection and Provision**: Trusting God means believing that He will protect them and provide for all their needs now and in the years to come.
- **Hope for Their Future**: When their future is entrusted to God, you can face challenges with hope, trusting that He will lead them in the right direction.
- **Spiritual Foundation**: Trusting the Lord reinforces your child's spiritual foundation, enabling them to grow in faith, wisdom, and character, especially when they are away from home.
- **Peace in Uncertainty**: In moments of worry or fear about their future, trusting God brings peace, knowing He is always in control.
- **Rest in His Timing**: Trusting God's timing allows you to release control, knowing that He will work all things together for your child's good in His perfect time.

The house is silent, except for the hum of the washer and dryer as I write this. I smile, gazing at a picture of the family my husband and I built together. We've come such a long way from the 22-year-old kids who fell in love. I know this is just the beginning because the best is yet to come!

# Epilogue:

No one warned me that my prayers would need to go deeper and be bolder when my kids went off to college. I expected their environment to be different from what they were used to because I remember what college was like. But the Gen Z version of college is an entirely different ball game. Still, I choose not to worry because, thank God, He is the same yesterday, today, and forevermore.

I've found myself in full-on spiritual warfare for my children. My prayers went from, *"Lord, please let my kids have a good year,"* to *"Satan, the Lord rebuke you!"* all within 24 hours. One issue after another came rushing in. It felt like I was battling nonstop. I couldn't sleep, I had no peace, and then even my younger kids seemed affected. They were dealing with friendship problems, bad attitudes, failing grades, and laziness. That's when I knew it wasn't just life; it was spiritual warfare.

In response, I did the one thing I knew would have the greatest impact: I turned to God's Word and began to pray. The most important gift I can ever give my children is prayer. No number of toys, clothes, or experiences can replace the power of prayer. When you add fasting, you tap into the Holy Spirit's power and partner with God to fight for your family. The Holy Spirit provides discernment and guides you to pray specific, tactical prayers that destroy the enemy's plans. I want to share some of those prayers with you in case the enemy tries to knock on your door too.

Now, according to Numbers 6:24-26: May the Lord bless you and keep you. May the Lord's face smile on you and be gracious to you. May the Lord show you His favor and give you His peace on this journey of parenthood.

You've got this! Keep praying, keep fighting, and keep trusting God every step of the way.

**Prayers for Your Children**

Anxious Thoughts

Change of Heart and Attitude

Confidence

Education

Focus

Forgiveness

Friendship

Health

Integrity

Joy

Laziness

Love of God

Mental health

Money

Negative talk

Obedience

Peace

Relationship with Jesus

Salvation

Spiritual Warfare

Suicide

Worldliness

# Anxious Thoughts

Dear Jesus, Encourage your child(ren) to align their hearts and minds with God's truth and remain steadfast against the enemy's deceptions. The enemy desires nothing more than to steal, kill, and destroy my child/children. He works through deception. Help my child/children to reject his lies. Your Word in John 10:10 says, *"The thief comes only to steal and kill and destroy. I came that they may have life and have it abundantly."* Help them to capture every thought and hold it up to You. Empower them to cast down any and all pretentious arguments that try to supersede the truth of the gospel, as instructed in 2 Corinthians 10:5. Guide them to think on things according to Your Word in Philippians 4:8, which says, *"Finally, brothers and sisters, whatever is true, whatever is noble, whatever is right, whatever is pure, whatever is lovely, whatever is admirable—if anything is excellent or praiseworthy—think about such things."*

Protect what enters their gates. Guard and filter everything that comes through their eye gates. Keep them from entertaining things they see that do not glorify You. As Matthew 6:22-23 teaches us, *"The eye is the lamp of the body. If your eyes are healthy, your whole body will be full of light. But if your eyes are unhealthy, your whole body will be full of darkness. If then the light within you is darkness, how great is that darkness!"* Help them to be strong and adhere to Psalm 101:3: *"I will not set before my eyes anything that is worthless. I hate the work of those who fall away; it shall not cling to me."*

Protect and filter what they choose to listen to. Guard their ear gates from perverse media, gossip, and all kinds of evil that the enemy tries to use to infiltrate their minds. Help them to live according to Proverbs 4:23: *"Above all else, guard your heart, for everything you do flows from it."* Please do not let evil enter their heart gates in the form of unforgiveness, hatred, idolatry, or jealousy.

Do not allow them to adopt the customs or thinking of the world, as taught in Romans 12:2: *"Do not conform to the pattern of this world, but be transformed by the renewing of your mind."* Help them to avoid loving the world, as stated in 1 John 2:15-17: *"Do not love the world or anything in the world. If anyone loves the world, love for the father is not in them. For everything in the world, the lust of the flesh, the lust of the eyes, and the pride of life comes not from the father but from the world. The world and its desires pass away, but whoever does the will of God lives forever."*

Instead, help them to be bold in character and stand firm, refusing to shrink back in order to fit in. Remind them, as we learn in 2 Timothy 1:7: *"For God gave us a spirit not of fear but of power and love and self-control."* Show them, Lord, that they are called to be a light. Let the Holy Spirit remind them of Your Word in Matthew 5:14-16, which says, *"You are the light of the world. A town built on a hill cannot be hidden. Neither do people light a lamp and put it under a bowl. Instead, they put it on its stand, and it gives light to everyone in the house. In the same way, let your light shine before others, that they may see your good deeds and glorify your Father in heaven."*

Thank You for hearing my prayer, in Jesus' name,

Amen.

*I understand this may seem lengthy, but through my experiences with patients, family members, and friends, I've witnessed firsthand how paralyzing anxiety can be.*

# Change of Heart and Attitude

Dear Lord, I come before You today, seeking Your wisdom and guidance in addressing the negative attitude of my child(ren). I ask that You remove all bitterness, anger, rage, harsh words, and negativity from their hearts. Replace these destructive tendencies with kindness, compassion, and forgiveness, just as You have forgiven us in Christ, as Ephesians 4:31-32 reminds us: *"Get rid of all bitterness, rage and anger, brawling and slander, along with every form of malice. Be kind and compassionate to one another, forgiving each other, just as in Christ God forgave you."* Lord, I pray that these qualities take root in my child(ren) so they may embody Your love and grace in their interactions with others.

Your Word in Proverbs 16:32 teaches us: *"Better a patient person than a warrior, one with self-control than one who takes a city."* Father, I ask that You bless my child(ren) with the strength and patience to regulate their emotions. Help them understand that true strength lies not in force but in remaining calm and composed, especially during challenging moments.

Lord, I know that through Christ, my child(ren) are made new. As 2 Corinthians 5:17 declares: *"Therefore, if anyone is in Christ, the new creation has come: The old has gone, the new is here!"* Help them embrace this new identity in You, turning away from old habits of deceitful speech, negativity, and harmful attitudes. Renew their minds and transform their hearts to reflect Your righteousness and holiness, as You have called them to be, as Ephesians 4:24 reminds us: *"Put on the new self, created to be like God in true righteousness and holiness."*

Finally, I ask that You bless my child(ren) with power, love, and self-discipline, as promised in 2 Timothy 1:7: *"For the Spirit God gave us does not make us timid, but gives us power, love, and self-discipline."* May they experience the fullness of Your Spirit, transforming their attitudes and actions to align with Christ's example.

In the precious name of Jesus, I pray,

Amen.

# Confidence

Dear Lord, Your Word tells us in Hebrews 10:35 not to throw away our confidence, for it will be richly rewarded. I pray that if my child(ren) have lost their confidence, you would restore it to them. Remind them of who they are in You. You have made my child(ren) lovely and altogether beautiful, as Psalm 139:14 declares: *"I praise You because I am fearfully and wonderfully made; Your works are wonderful, I know that full well."* They were wonderfully made by Your hands and are precious in Your sight.

Lord, help my child(ren) to see all that You have created them to be. They are the righteousness of God through Christ Jesus, as 2 Corinthians 5:21 reminds us: *"God made Him who had no sin to be sin for us, so that in Him we might become the righteousness of God."* They are complete in You, lacking nothing, as Colossians 2:10 says: "And in Christ you have been brought to fullness. He is the head over every power and authority." They are joint heirs with Christ, as Romans 8:17 assures us: *"Now if we are children, then we are heirs—heirs of God and co-heirs with Christ."*

Help my child(ren) to believe they are capable of great things as they place their trust in You. As Philippians 4:13 declares: *"I can do all this through Him who gives me strength."* Restore their confidence and help them to walk boldly in the identity You have given them. May they reclaim their confidence and receive the reward You have promised.

May they be encouraged by knowing there is a great cloud of witnesses cheering them on, as Hebrews 12:1 says: *"Therefore, since we are surrounded by such a great cloud of witnesses, let us throw off everything that hinders and the sin that so easily entangles. And let us run with perseverance the race marked out for us."* Lord, help them to keep their eyes fixed on You, the author and perfecter of their faith, as Hebrews 12:2 reminds us: *"Fixing our eyes on Jesus, the pioneer and perfecter of faith."*

Thank You, Heavenly Father, for hearing my prayer. I trust that You are working in the hearts of my child(ren).
In Jesus Christ's name, I pray,
Amen

# Education

Dear Lord, Thank You for the gift of my child(ren)'s minds and their ability to learn. I pray they would have the mindset of Christ, as Your Word says in Philippians 2:5: *"Let this mind be in you which was also in Christ Jesus."* I ask for godly thinking to guide them and for godly teachers to help facilitate their learning. Help me, as their parent, to be their first teacher at home, teaching them about You every day.\

Lord, give me wisdom to work alongside those entrusted with my child(ren)'s education. If my child(ren) need wisdom, I pray they would turn to You, as James 1:5 promises: *"If any of you lacks wisdom, let him ask of God, who gives to all liberally and without reproach, and it will be given to him."*

Instruct our children, Lord, according to Your thoughts and purposes, as 1 Corinthians 2:16 declares: *"But we have the mind of Christ."* May their efforts be blessed and successful, as Psalm 90:17 says: *"Let the favor of the Lord our God be upon us, and establish the work of our hands."*

Thank You for being present in every lesson, paper, project, and test. Make their learning environment conducive

to growth, filled with Your peace and guidance. Bless everyone my child(ren) comes into contact with today, and keep them safe and secure, with their minds fixed on You, as Isaiah 26:3 assures us: *"You will keep in perfect peace those whose minds are steadfast, because they trust in You."*
In Jesus' name, I pray,
Amen

# Focus

Dear Lord, I pray for Your guidance in the life of my child(ren), as Your Word promises that You will direct their paths, as stated in Proverbs 3:5-6: *"Trust in the Lord with all your heart and lean not on your own understanding; in all your ways submit to Him, and He will make your paths straight."* Please help them stay focused on their studies and work, as Your Word instructs us in Colossians 3:23: *"Whatever you do, work at it with all your heart, as working for the Lord, not for human masters."* Grant them clarity of thought so they may think on things that are lovely, pure, and true, as Philippians 4:8 reminds us: *"Finally, brothers and sisters, whatever is true, whatever is noble, whatever is right, whatever is pure, whatever is lovely, whatever is admirable—if anything is excellent or praiseworthy—think about such things."* Guard their minds and help them test and approve what Your will is for their lives, just as Romans 12:2 calls us to do: *"Do not conform to the pattern of this world, but be transformed by the renewing of your mind. Then you will be able to test and approve what God's will is—His good, pleasing and perfect will.*

I pray that my child(ren) will not be distracted by the things of this world but will remain mindful of what is most important. Help them prioritize their day and walk in wisdom, as Ephesians 5:15-16 encourages: *"Be very careful, then, how you live not as unwise but as wise, making the most of every opportunity, because the days are evil."* I declare that any traps set by the enemy to steal, kill, and destroy the purpose and plans You have for their lives be broken and undone in Jesus' name, as John 10:10 states: *"The thief comes only to steal and kill and destroy; I have come that they may have life and have it to the full."*

I pray that my child(ren) walk boldly in the calling You have placed on their lives, just as You called Jeremiah from the womb, as Jeremiah 1:5 reminds us: *"Before I formed you in the womb I knew you, before you were born I set you apart; I appointed you as a prophet to the nations."* Send Your angels to guard them, as Psalm 91:11 promises: *"For He will command His angels concerning you to guard you in all your ways." Keep them from stumbling, guide their footsteps, as Psalm 37:23 declares:* "The Lord makes firm the steps of the one who delights in Him." Set a watch over their lips, as Psalm 141:3 says: *"Set a guard over my mouth, Lord; keep watch over the door of my lips."* Remove anyone from their lives who is not meant to accompany them on their journey, letting them lose interest and fall away.

Help them always to look to You, knowing that their help comes from the Lord, the Maker of heaven and earth, as Psalm 121:1-2 assures us: *"I lift up my eyes to the mountains where does my help come from? My help comes from the Lord, the Maker of heaven and earth."*
In Jesus' name, I pray,

Amen

# Forgiveness

Heavenly Father, I come before You today, thanking You for the gift of my child(ren)'s lives and for Your hand upon them. I pray that You would guide them in the way of forgiveness—both in receiving and offering it. Lord, help them to understand that forgiveness is not just a command but a blessing that frees us from the chains of bitterness and anger. Teach them, as Your Word says in Ephesians 4:32: *"Be kind and compassionate to one another, forgiving each other, just as in Christ God forgave you."* Let them not hold onto grudges but instead grant them the strength to release all offenses into Your hands.

Help them to remember Your forgiveness, as 1 John 1:9 reminds us: *"If we confess our sins, He is faithful and just to forgive us our sins and to cleanse us from all unrighteousness."* May they experience the joy of being forgiven by You and be inspired to extend that same grace to others.

Lord, when they face hurt or betrayal, remind them of Matthew 18:21-22, where Jesus teaches us to forgive not just seven times but seventy-seven times: *"Then Peter came to Jesus and asked, 'Lord, how many times shall I forgive my brother or sister who sins against me? Up to seven times?' Jesus answered, 'I tell you, not seven times, but seventy-seven times.'"* Let their hearts remain soft, their spirits humble, and their minds free of the need for revenge or bitterness.

Fill them with Your peace, as Philippians 4:7 promises: *"And the peace of God, which transcends all understanding, will guard your hearts and your minds in Christ Jesus."* May they not be consumed by unforgiveness but instead rest in Your peace, allowing Your love to flow through them.

Finally, I pray that my child(ren) grow in their understanding of Your great love, which covers all sins, as 1 Peter 4:8 says: *"Above all, love each other deeply, because love covers over a multitude of sins."* May they walk in the freedom that comes with forgiving others, just as You have forgiven them.

In Jesus' mighty name, I pray,

Amen.

# Friendship

Lord, Thank You for being closer than a brother to my child(ren), as Proverbs 18:24 reminds us: *"One who has unreliable friends soon comes to ruin, but there is a friend who sticks closer than a brother."* I pray that You surround them with friends who love them as You do. May they find friends who sharpen them, as Proverbs 27:17 says: *"As iron sharpens iron, so one person sharpens another."* Surround them with friends who encourage them to grow in their faith and character.

I ask for friends who are truthful, full of integrity, loyal, driven, focused, and caring. May they have friends who speak the truth in love, call them out when they are wrong, and fear You above all, as Ephesians 4:15 reminds us: *"Instead, speaking the truth in love, we will grow to become in every respect the mature body of Him who is the head, that is, Christ."* And as Proverbs 12:1 teaches: *"Whoever loves discipline loves knowledge, but whoever hates correction is stupid."*

Lord, I desire for my child(ren) to have friends who draw them closer to You. Help them to be good friends in return—showing kindness, loyalty, and love—and protect them from those who may mean them harm or who do not value themselves or my child(ren). Your Word in 1 Corinthians 15:33 says: *"Do not be misled: 'Bad company corrupts good character.'"* I pray that my child(ren) will be surrounded by people who build them up, not tear them down.

Thank You, Lord, for being our best friend first, as John 15:13 declares: *"Greater love has no one than this: to lay down one's life for one's friends."* We love You, honor You, and trust You with every part of our lives. I also pray that when my child(ren) reach adulthood, they will continue to develop friendships that reflect Your love and truth.

In Jesus' name, I pray,

Amen

# Health

Lord, we thank You that, as Your beloved, You have promised to prosper us and keep us in good health, just as our souls prosper, as 3 John 1:2 reminds us: *"Dear friend, I pray that you may enjoy good health and that all may go well with you, even as your soul is getting along well."* We ask that You prosper our minds, wills, and emotions, bringing them into perfect health. Thank You for the health of our bodies and for everything functioning in divine order. Bless the food we eat; purify and sanctify it, removing any impurities, in Jesus' name.

If there is any illness present, whether known or unknown, we command the spirit of infirmity to leave our children's bodies now, in the name of Jesus. You are our Healer, Jehovah Rapha, and we trust you to heal as only You can. Whether through a supernatural touch or through medicine, we bless the healing process and the hands of those caring for our children. May You overturn every bed of sickness and replace it with strength and vitality.

We receive our healing with joy and gratitude, knowing that by Your stripes, our children are healed, as Isaiah 53:5 declares: *"But He was pierced for our transgressions, He was crushed for our iniquities; the punishment that brought us peace was on Him, and by His wounds we are healed."* We thank You in advance for Your faithfulness and unfailing love.

In Jesus' mighty name, I pray,

Amen

# Integrity

God, I truly thank You for the gift of our child(ren). We ask that You help them walk in truth and integrity in all things. Your Word says in Proverbs 12:22: *"The Lord detests lying lips, but He delights in people who are trustworthy."* We pray that You instill in them a deep love for truth and honesty, and that they would always choose to speak and live truthfully, even when it's difficult.

We ask that You expose any areas of deceit or secrecy and bring them into the light. Let our children understand the value of transparency and the freedom that comes with living in the light, as Your Word says in John 8:32: *"Then you will know the truth, and the truth will set you free."*

If there are any tendencies to sneak around or hide things, we pray that You reveal them and help our children choose honesty and openness instead. Surround them with Your wisdom and understanding so they may always walk in the light of Your truth.

We trust that You are shaping them into individuals of strong character, and we thank You for Your guidance in their lives. May their hearts be inclined to seek truth, and may their actions reflect Your righteousness.

In Jesus' name,

Amen

# Joy

Dear Lord, I come before You today, asking that You fill my child(ren) with Your joy. May Your joy overflow in their hearts, and may the fruit of Your Spirit be evident in their lives, especially during both triumphs and struggles. In the good times, may they rejoice with grateful hearts, and in difficult moments, may they find strength in Your presence. Let them remember that this is the day You have made, and may they rejoice and be glad in it, as Psalm 118:24 declares: *"The Lord has done it this very day; let us rejoice today and be glad."*

Lord, bless them with a joyful heart that delights in You, knowing that You are a good and faithful God who strengthens them with Your joy, as Nehemiah 8:10 reminds us: *"Do not grieve, for the joy of the Lord is your strength."* Help them to focus on You throughout their day. Remind them that when Peter began to sink, it was because he took his eyes off Jesus and focused on the storm around him. Help them, too, to keep their eyes fixed on You, the One whom even the winds and the sea obey, as Matthew 8:27 reveals: *"The men were amazed and asked, 'What kind of man is this? Even the winds and the waves obey Him!'"*

Teach them to bring all their worries and cares before You, as 1 Peter 5:7 encourages: *"Cast all your anxiety on Him because He cares for you."* May they experience Your peace and joy today, and may this joy sustain them in the days to come. Let Your love and presence be the source of their strength, and may they find true and lasting joy in You, their Savior.

In Jesus' name, I pray,

Amen

# The Love of God

Dear Heavenly Father, You are love, and Your love is immeasurable. As 1 John 4:8 reminds us: *"Whoever does not love does not know God, because God is love."* Lord, I pray that my child(ren) would experience the fullness of Your love in their lives. May they come to know the depth, height, and width of Your love, which surpasses all understanding, as Ephesians 3:17-19 declares: *"So that Christ may dwell in your hearts through faith. And I pray that you, being rooted and established in love, may have power, together with all the Lord's holy people, to grasp how wide and long and high and deep is the love of Christ, and to know this love that surpasses knowledge—that you may be filled to the measure of all the fullness of God."*

Father, you sent Your Son to die for my child(ren), and I pray they will come to fully understand and believe in that sacrificial love, as John 3:16 affirms: *"For God so loved the world that He gave His one and only Son, that whoever believes in Him shall not perish but have eternal life."* Help my child(ren) to trust in the One who was sent to save them and to realize that nothing is more powerful than the love You have for them.

Lord, help my child(ren) to grasp that no power on earth can separate them from Your love, as Romans 8:38-39 assures us: *"For I am convinced that neither death nor life, neither angels nor demons, neither the present nor the future, nor any powers, neither height nor depth, nor anything else in all creation, will be able to separate us from the love of God that is in Christ Jesus our Lord."*

I also pray that my child(ren) will come to know that Your love drives out all fear, as 1 John 4:18 says: *"There is no fear in love. But perfect love drives out fear, because fear has to do with punishment. The one who fears is not made perfect in love."* May Your perfect love surround them, filling their hearts with peace and security, knowing they are deeply loved by You.

Thank You, Father, for Your love that never fails. I trust that You will reveal Your love in mighty ways to my child(ren), and that they will rest in the assurance that they are deeply loved by You.

In Jesus' name, I pray,

Amen

# Laziness

Dear Lord, Thank You for the diligence You've instilled in my child(ren). In the name of Jesus, I come against the spirit of laziness and pray that each of my children will remain diligent to the very end so that all they hope for spiritually and physically will come to pass. You are a just God who promises not to forget their work, as Hebrews 6:10 reminds us: *"God is not unjust; He will not forget your work and the love you have shown Him as you have helped His people and continue to help them."* I ask that You help my child(ren) to work with passion and excellence in everything they do, avoiding laziness and always giving their best, as Hebrews 6:10-12 encourages: *"We want each of you to show this same diligence to the very end, so that what you hope for may be fully realized. We do not want you to become lazy, but to imitate those who through faith and patience inherit what has been promised."*

Throughout Your Word, we see examples of hard work and progress—from Adam to Ezra to Jesus. You declared in Proverbs 12:24: *"Diligent hands will rule, but laziness ends in forced labor."* I pray that my child(ren) will always be productive, moving forward with purpose. I also ask that You teach them the balance between productivity and rest, so they may honor You with both their work and their rest.

  Bless them, Lord, to keep pressing forward in all they do, knowing that You are with them every step of the way. In Jesus' name, I pray.

Amen

# Mental Health

Lord, We come before You in gratitude for the precious gift of our children. We thank You that You are their Creator, and You have formed them with a purpose and a future full of hope. We pray for their mental health today, asking that You guard their minds and hearts with Your peace, as Philippians 4:7 promises: *"And the peace of God, which transcends all understanding, will guard your hearts and your minds in Christ Jesus."*

We declare that their minds are not conformed to the patterns of this world but are transformed by the renewing of their thoughts, as Romans 12:2 instructs: *"Do not conform to the pattern of this world, but be transformed by the renewing of your mind. Then you will be able to test and approve what God's will is—His good, pleasing and perfect will."* Lord, protect them from negative influences, fear, anxiety, chemical imbalances, and confusion. Fill their minds with truth, love, and peace, and let Your Word be a lamp to their feet and a light to their path, as Psalm 119:105 declares: *"Your word is a lamp to my feet and a light to my path."*

We pray for clarity of thought, soundness of mind, and strength in their emotions. Where there is worry or stress, we ask that Your presence bring calm. We break the spirit of depression, anxiety, and any mental stronghold that tries to bind them, and we speak Your freedom over their minds in the mighty name of Jesus.

We thank You for the assurance in Isaiah 26:3: *"You will keep in perfect peace those whose minds are steadfast, because they trust in You."* We declare that our children will place their full trust in You, and that Your peace will guard their hearts and minds. We ask that You send them help in the form of prayer partners and wise counsel. Holy Spirit, bless their souls and lead them to walk faithfully in Your ways.

In Jesus' name, I pray,

Amen

# Money

Jehovah Jireh, Thank You for the abundant blessings You provide. The earth is Yours and everything in it, as Psalm 24:1 declares: *"The earth is the Lord's, and everything in it, the world, and all who live in it."* Because of this, we need not worry about what we will eat, drink, or wear, for life is more than these things. As Matthew 6:25 reminds us: "Therefore I tell you, do not worry about your life, what you will eat or drink; or about your body, what you will wear. Is not life more than food, and the body more than clothes?" You already know our needs, and we trust you to provide for us, casting all our cares upon You. Instead of worrying, we will seek Your kingdom first, live righteously, and trust that everything we need will be given to us, as Matthew 6:31-33 assures: *"So do not worry, saying, 'What shall we eat?' or 'What shall we drink?' or 'What shall we wear?' For the pagans run after all these things, and your heavenly Father knows that you need them. But seek first His kingdom and His righteousness, and all these things will be given to you as well."*

Lord, bless my child(ren) to be a blessing to others. Let their hearts always be generous, for You said it is more blessed to give than to receive, as Acts 20:35 reminds us: *"In everything I did, I showed you that by this kind of hard work we must help the weak, remembering the words the Lord Jesus Himself said: 'It is more blessed to give than to receive.'"* Remind them to give to the poor, as Proverbs 19:17 declares: "Whoever is kind to the poor lends to the Lord, and He will reward them for what they have done." Teach them not to place their trust in riches, as Psalm 62:10 warns: *"Do not trust in extortion or put vain hope in stolen goods; though your riches increase, do not set your heart on them."* Keep them free from the love of money, and help them to be content with what they have. Thank You for the promise in Hebrews 13:5-6: *"Never will I leave you; never will I forsake you. So, we say with confidence, 'The Lord is my helper; I will not be afraid. What can mere mortals do to me?'"*

I pray that You protect them from the temptation of quick riches and teach them to be wise in their finances. Your Word tells us in Proverbs 13:11: *"Dishonest money dwindles away, but whoever gathers money little by little makes it grow."* Let them commit their work to You, Lord, so that their plans may be established, as Proverbs 16:3 instructs: *"Commit to the Lord whatever you do, and He will establish your plans."* Help them to trust You in the process toward prosperity.

Lord, I also pray that our children will be faithful stewards of the gifts, talents, and resources You've entrusted to them, as 1 Peter 4:10 says: *"Each of you should use whatever gift you have received to serve others, as faithful stewards of God's grace in its various forms."* Whether in their work, household responsibilities, or studies, let them be diligent and faithful, as 1 Corinthians 4:2 reminds us: *"Now it is required that those who have been given a trust must prove faithful."* Reveal to them that in everything they do, they are working for You. Let them remember Colossians 3:23-24: *"Whatever you do, work at it with all your heart, as working for the Lord, not for human masters, since you know that you will receive an inheritance from the Lord as a reward. It is the Lord Christ you are serving."*

In Jesus' name, I pray,

Amen

# Negative Speech

Heavenly Father, Your Word teaches us in Proverbs 18:21: *"The tongue has the power of life and death, and those who love it will eat its fruit."* We ask You to guide and encourage our child(ren) to speak life over themselves, knowing that they will have what they say, as Mark 11:23 reminds us: *"Truly I tell you, if anyone says to this mountain, 'Go, throw yourself into the sea,' and does not doubt in their heart but believes that what they say will happen, it will be done for them."* Protect them from speaking words of death, despair, or negativity over their lives. Set a guard over their mouths, as Psalm 141:3 instructs: *"Set a guard over my mouth, Lord; keep watch over the door of my lips."*

Holy Spirit, remind them not to speak foolishly, as Proverbs 6:2 warns: *"You have been trapped by what you said, ensnared by the words of your mouth."* Help them understand that, as Proverbs 15:2 teaches: *"The tongue of the wise adorns knowledge, but the mouth of the fool gushes folly."* Keep them from inviting strife or harm through their speech. Instead, let their words be righteous, for Proverbs 10:31 says: *"From the mouth of the righteous comes the fruit of wisdom, but a perverse tongue will be silenced."* May their speech be a source of encouragement, as Proverbs 10:21 declares: *"The lips of the righteous nourish many, but fools die for lack of sense."*

Lord, fill their lives with good things from the fruit of their lips, as Proverbs 12:14 promises: *"From the fruit of their lips people are filled with good things, and the work of their hands brings them reward."* Teach them to speak thoughtfully, as Proverbs 15:28 says: *"The heart of the righteous weighs its answers, but the mouth of the wicked gushes evil."* May their words be gracious, as Proverbs 16:24 reminds us: *"Gracious words are a honeycomb, sweet to the soul and healing to the bones."* Help them always respond with a gentle answer in conflict, knowing it will turn away wrath, as Proverbs 15:1 declares: *"A gentle answer turns away wrath, but a harsh word stirs up anger."*

Teach them the wisdom of knowing when to speak and when to remain silent, for Proverbs 10:19 warns: *"Sin is not ended by multiplying words, but the prudent hold their tongues."* Help them understand that, as Proverbs 21:23 states: *"Those who guard their mouths and their tongues keep themselves from calamity."* Protect them from lying and gossip, as Proverbs 10:18 cautions: *"Whoever conceals hatred with lying lips and spreads slander is a fool."*

Finally, let their speech be sweet as they speak life to themselves and others.

In Jesus' name, I pray,

Amen

# Obedience

**D**ear Heavenly Father, I come before You today, lifting up my child(ren) and asking for Your guidance in their lives. I pray that You would teach them the importance of obedience—both to You and to those in authority over them. Your Word says in Ephesians 6:1: *"Children, obey your parents in the Lord, for this is right."* Help them to understand the value of honoring and respecting their parents, as well as those placed in positions of leadership over them.

Lord, let them remember that obedience is not just an outward action but a matter of the heart. Help them to obey with a cheerful spirit, as Colossians 3:23 reminds us: *"Whatever you do, work at it with all your heart, as working for the Lord, not for human masters."* May their hearts be aligned with Your will so they follow Your commands with love and reverence.

Teach them to obey with a spirit of humility, as Your Word tells us in James 4:10: *"Humble yourselves before the Lord, and He will lift you up."* Let them recognize that obedience brings blessing, as Proverbs 3:1-2 declares: *"My son, do not forget my teaching, but keep my commands in your heart, for they will prolong your life many years and bring you peace and prosperity."*

Father, help my children understand that obedience is an expression of their love for You. As John 14:15 states: *"If you love me, keep my commands."* May they grow to trust in Your perfect wisdom, knowing that You have good plans for them, as Jeremiah 29:11 assures us: *"For I know the plans I have for you... plans to prosper you and not to harm you, plans to give you hope and a future."* Let their obedience be a reflection of their faith in You so that others may see Your work in their lives and give You glory.

I also pray that they would obey with a spirit of joy and not reluctance. Let their hearts be full of love for You and for those You have placed in their lives, and may they walk in obedience not out of obligation but out of love for You.

Thank You, Lord, for Your faithfulness in shaping and guiding my children. May they grow in wisdom and understanding as they learn to walk in obedience to You and to those around them.

In Jesus' name, I pray,

Amen

# Peace

Dear Heavenly Father, I come before You with a heart full of love and care for my children. I pray that You would surround them with Your peace that transcends all understanding, as Your Word promises in Philippians 4:7: *"And the peace of God, which transcends all understanding, will guard your hearts and your minds in Christ Jesus."* Lord, I ask that You fill their hearts with Your peace, especially when they face challenges, fear, or confusion. Let them remember that You are the Prince of Peace, as Isaiah 9:6 declares: *"For to us a child is born, to us a son is given... and He will be called Wonderful Counselor, Mighty God, Everlasting Father, Prince of Peace."* You are always with them, bringing calm in the midst of any storm. May they find comfort in Your presence, knowing that You will keep in perfect peace those whose minds are steadfast because they trust in You, as Isaiah 26:3 assures: *"You will keep in perfect peace those whose minds are steadfast, because they trust in You."*

Help them to trust in You fully, knowing that You are their refuge and strength, a very present help in times of trouble, as Psalm 46:1 reminds us: *"God is our refuge and strength, an ever-present help in trouble."* Let them feel Your peace in their hearts, even in moments of anxiety or restlessness, as You have said in Philippians 4:6-7: *"Do not be anxious about anything, but in every situation, by prayer and petition, with thanksgiving, present your requests to God. And the peace of God, which transcends all understanding, will guard your hearts and your minds in Christ Jesus."*

Lord, I pray that You would teach them to be peacemakers, as Jesus said in Matthew 5:9: *"Blessed are the peacemakers, for they will be called children of God."* Help them reflect Your peace in their relationships, being slow to anger and quick to forgive. Let them pursue peace with all people, as Hebrews 12:14 instructs: *"Make every effort to live in peace with everyone and to be holy; without holiness no one will see the Lord."* When they face difficult situations or conflicts, give them the strength to respond with Your peace, knowing that peace is a fruit of the Spirit, as Galatians 5:22 reminds us: *"But the fruit of the Spirit is love, joy, peace, forbearance, kindness, goodness, faithfulness..."* May they always remember that they are never alone, for You are with them, guiding them in paths of peace.

I thank You, Lord, for Your faithfulness to my child(ren), and I trust that You will continue to surround them with Your peace in every circumstance. May their lives be a reflection of Your peace, bringing glory to Your name. In Jesus' name, I pray,
Amen

# Relationship with Jesus

Dear Lord, I lift my child(ren) before You and pray that You bless them with a deep, intimate relationship with Jesus. May they come to know their true identity in Christ, for Your Word says in 2 Corinthians 5:17: *"If anyone is in Christ, he is a new creation; the old has gone, the new has come."* Let them experience the fellowship of Your Spirit, finding peace that surpasses all understanding, as it is written in John 14:27: *"Peace I leave with you; my peace I give you. I do not give to you as the world gives. Do not let your hearts be troubled and do not be afraid."* Fill their hearts with Your love, for we know from 1 John 4:19: *"We love because He first loved us."*

I pray that they will accept the free gift of salvation and forever lean on the arm of the Lord, knowing that, as Isaiah 59:1 reminds us: *"Surely the arm of the Lord is not too short to save, nor His ear too dull to hear."* Hear their cry, Lord, for You are near to those who call on You. As Psalm 34:17 declares: *"The righteous cry out, and the Lord hears them; He delivers them from all their troubles."* You see them when they rise and when they rest, as it is written in

Psalm 121:5: *"The Lord watches over you; the Lord is your shade at your right hand."*

Pour out Your Spirit upon them so that they may know You and the power of Your resurrection, as Philippians 3:10 speaks of: *"I want to know Christ—yes, to know the power of His resurrection and participation in His sufferings, becoming like Him in His death."* Renew their minds in Christ Jesus, and may they be transformed by the renewing of their thoughts, as Your Word declares in Romans 12:2: *"Do not conform to the pattern of this world, but be transformed by the renewing of your mind. Then you will be able to test and approve what God's will is—His good, pleasing, and perfect will."* Help them to believe for more and to hope for Your glory to be evident in their lives, knowing that, as Isaiah 40:31 assures us: *"Those who hope in the Lord will renew their strength. They will soar on wings like eagles; they will run and not grow weary; they will walk and not be faint."*

Touch their hearts, Lord, that they may seek Your forgiveness for their sins and live righteously before You. As 1 John 1:9 reminds us: *"If we confess our sins, He is faithful and just and will forgive us our sins and purify us from all unrighteousness."* May their lives reflect the light of

Christ, so that others may see their good works and glorify our Father in heaven, as Matthew 5:16 declares: *"Let your light shine before others, that they may see your good deeds and glorify your Father in heaven."*

Bless them to be fishers of men, as You called Your disciples to be in Matthew 4:19: *"Come, follow me," Jesus said, "and I will send you out to fish for people."* Guide them in their walk as they follow You, their Good Shepherd, as John 10:11 proclaims: "I am the good shepherd. The good shepherd lays down His life for the sheep."

Let them grow more in love with You each day, knowing, as 1 John 4:19 tells us: *"We love because He first loved us."*

In Jesus' name, I pray,

Amen

# Salvation

Dear Heavenly Father, I come before You with a heart full of faith and hope for my children. Lord, I pray that You would draw them near to You, and that they would come to know the precious gift of salvation through Jesus Christ. Your Word says in John 3:16: *"For God so loved the world that He gave His one and only Son, that whoever believes in Him shall not perish but have eternal life."* I pray that my children would embrace this truth and put their trust in Jesus as their Savior.

Father, open their hearts to the gospel message. As Your Word says in Romans 10:9: *"If you declare with your mouth, 'Jesus is Lord,' and believe in your heart that God raised Him from the dead, you will be saved."* I pray that they would confess with their mouths and believe in their hearts in the saving power of Jesus Christ. Let them know, as Acts 4:12 declares: *"Salvation is found in no one else, for there is no other name under heaven given to mankind by which we must be saved."* Help them to understand that Jesus is the only way, the truth, and the life, as John 14:6 assures us: *"I am the way and the truth and the life. No one comes to the father except through me."*

Lord, I ask that You would give them a heart of repentance, as Your Word says in 2 Peter 3:9: *"The Lord is not slow in keeping His promise, as some understand slowness. Instead, He is patient with you, not wanting anyone to perish, but everyone to come to repentance."* Help them to understand the weight of their sins and the freedom that comes through Jesus' death, burial, and resurrection. May they come to You in humility, asking for forgiveness and accepting the gift of eternal life, as 1 John 1:9 reminds us: *"If we confess our sins, He is faithful and just and will forgive us our sins and purify us from all unrighteousness."*

I pray that they would be filled with the Holy Spirit, who helps them live in accordance with Your will and empowers them to walk in the newness of life that salvation brings. As Romans 8:11 declares: *"And if the Spirit of Him who raised Jesus from the dead is living in you, He who raised Christ from the dead will also give life to your mortal bodies because of His Spirit who lives in you."* Let them experience the joy of salvation and the peace that comes from knowing they are secure in Christ, as Romans 5:1 assures us: *"Therefore, since we have been justified through faith, we have peace with God through our Lord Jesus Christ."*

Lord, I also pray that they would grow in their understanding of Your love and grace, and that they would live out their salvation by loving others and sharing the good news of Jesus with the world. Your Word in Ephesians 2:8-9 reminds us: *"For it is by grace you have been saved, through faith—and this is not from yourselves, it is the gift of God—not by works, so that no one can boast."* May they always remember that salvation is a gift, not something they can earn, but a demonstration of Your incredible love.

I thank You, Lord, for the gift of eternal life through Jesus Christ. I pray that my children would come to know You intimately and experience the fullness of Your grace and salvation.

In Jesus' name, I pray,

Amen

# Spiritual Warfare

Dear Heavenly Father, I come before You with a heart full of love and concern for my children. I pray that You would surround them with Your protection and cover them with Your mighty hand as they face the battles of this world, both seen and unseen. Your Word tells us in Ephesians 6:11: *"Put on the full armor of God, so that you can take your stand against the devil's schemes."* I pray that my children would be equipped with Your armor—truth, righteousness, the gospel of peace, faith, salvation, the sword of the Spirit, which is Your Word, and prayer.

Lord, I know that spiritual warfare is real and that our enemy seeks to devour and deceive. As 1 Peter 5:8 warns us: *"Be alert and of sober mind. Your enemy the devil prowls around like a roaring lion looking for someone to devour."* I pray that You would make my children aware of the spiritual battles around them. Help them to stand firm in their faith, trusting in Your promise that "greater is He who is in you than he who is in the world" (1 John 4:4). May they always lean on Your strength and not their own, knowing that You are their refuge and fortress, as Psalm 91:2 declares: *"I will say of the Lord, 'He is my refuge and my fortress, my God, in whom I trust.'"*

Lord, I ask that You would guide my children in the way of truth and protect their minds from the lies and distractions of the enemy. Help them to recognize temptation when it comes and to resist it with Your Word, just as Jesus did in the wilderness (Matthew 4:1-11). May they be grounded in Your truth, knowing, as John 8:32 reminds us: *"Then you will know the truth, and the truth will set you free."* Let them hold onto the promise that *"no weapon formed against them shall prosper"* (Isaiah 54:17).

I pray that You would instill in them a heart of prayer, so that they would seek You in times of struggle and know, as James 5:16 assures us: *"The prayer of a righteous person is powerful and effective."* Teach them to be diligent in their spiritual practices—praying, reading Your Word, and walking in Your ways—so that they may resist the enemy and remain steadfast in their faith.

Father, I ask that You would bind any strongholds in their lives and break any chains of fear, doubt, or confusion. Replace them with Your peace that surpasses all understanding, as Philippians 4:7 promises: *"And the peace of God, which transcends all understanding, will guard your hearts and your minds in Christ Jesus."*

We claim the promise that You will keep them always. Thank You in advance for Your faithfulness and for hearing my prayer.

In Jesus' name, I pray,

Amen

# Suicide

Heavenly Father, We come before You today with hearts full of concern and love for the children in our lives. Lord, we know that You care deeply for each child, and Your Word reminds us that You have a purpose for their lives, filled with hope and a future. We lift up all children who are struggling with feelings of hopelessness, pain, and despair. We rebuke the spirit of suicide in the name of Jesus. Your Word says in Psalm 139:16: *"All the days ordained for me were written in Your book before one of them came to be."* Lord, keep our children from disrupting the plans You have so lovingly crafted for their lives. Surround them with Your peace, comfort, and love. May they always remember that they are precious in Your sight, created in Your image, and loved beyond measure. In moments when darkness clouds their hearts, let them hear Your voice speaking truth—that they are never alone and that You are always with them.

Father, we pray that You would send compassionate and understanding people into their lives—those who will listen, help, and point them toward the hope that is found in You. May they never forget Your promise in Jeremiah

29:11: *"For I know the plans I have for you," declares the Lord, "plans to prosper you and not to harm you, plans to give you hope and a future."* Lord, for those children overwhelmed by life's struggles, may they find refuge in Your presence. As Psalm 34:18 reminds us: *"The Lord is close to the brokenhearted and saves those who are crushed in spirit."* Let them feel Your nearness and trust that You will carry them through every storm.

We ask that You bind up the wounds of every child suffering emotionally or mentally. Help them find strength in Philippians 4:13, believing: *"I can do all this through Him who gives me strength."* Teach them to lean on You when they feel weak and remind them that, in Your hands, there is always a way forward.

Lord, we trust in Your promise in Psalm 147:3: *"He heals the brokenhearted and binds up their wounds."* We pray that Your healing touch will rest upon the hearts of every child who is suffering. Restore their joy, peace, and hope, and let them walk confidently in the knowledge of Your unfailing love.

Finally, Lord, we ask for wisdom and strength for parents, caregivers, and all who care for these children. May they be true representatives of Your love, offering comfort and support. Guide them by Your Holy Spirit to provide the help these children need in the most meaningful ways.

In Jesus' name, I pray,

Amen

# Worldliness

Heavenly Father, we come before You with hearts full of gratitude and concern for the children You have entrusted to us. Thank You for the precious gift of life and the unique purpose You have placed within each child. You have called them to be set apart, to reflect Your goodness, truth, and love in all they do.

Lord, we ask for Your protection over their hearts and minds, guarding them from the distractions and temptations of this world. In a culture that often encourages selfishness, materialism, and fleeting pleasures, help them to fix their eyes on You, the true source of joy and peace. Strengthen them to stand firm in their faith, as Romans 12:2 reminds us: *"Do not conform to the pattern of this world, but be transformed by the renewing of your mind."* May their thoughts, actions, and choices be rooted in Your Word rather than in the passing trends or pressures around them.

We know, Father, that this world offers many things that can lead them astray, but You have called them to a higher purpose. As 1 John 2:15-16 warns: *"Do not love the world or anything in the world. If anyone loves the world, love for the father is not in them. For everything in the* world—*the lust of the flesh, the lust of the eyes, and the pride of life—comes not from the father but from the world."* Protect their hearts from these temptations, and help them to find their true worth and identity in You alone.

Lord, we ask that You would fill their hearts with a deep love for Your Word. May it be a lamp to their feet and a light to their path, as Psalm 119:105 declares: *"Your word is a lamp for my feet, a light on my path."* Teach them that true joy and contentment are not found in worldly things but in living in Your presence and walking according to Your will.

Help them embrace Your calling to be salt and light in this world, as Matthew 5:14-16 says*: "You are the light of the world. A town built on a hill cannot be hidden. Neither do people light a lamp and put it under a bowl. Instead, they put it on its stand, and it gives light to everyone in the house."* May their lives shine brightly, reflecting Your love and truth to those around them.

Lord, we pray that You would cultivate in them hearts that hunger and thirst for righteousness. May they seek first Your Kingdom, as Matthew 6:33 encourages us: *"But seek first his kingdom and his righteousness, and all these things will be given to you as well."* Draw them toward the things that honor You, and fill them with the peace that comes from living in Your will.

Finally, we ask for wisdom, discernment, and strength for all those who influence our children—parents, teachers, mentors, and leaders. May they guide them with love, truth, and wisdom, always pointing them toward You, the source of all hope and transformation.

In Jesus' name, I pray,

Amen

www.ingramcontent.com/pod-product-compliance
Lightning Source LLC
Chambersburg PA
CBHW022110090426
42743CB00008B/797